Once Upon A Dream

Echoes Within

Edited By Lynsey Evans

First published in Great Britain in 2024 by:

YoungWriters
Est. 1991

Young Writers
Remus House
Coltsfoot Drive
Peterborough
PE2 9BF
Telephone: 01733 890066
Website: www.youngwriters.co.uk

All Rights Reserved
Book Design by Ashley Janson
© Copyright Contributors 2024
Softback ISBN 978-1-83565-408-8
Printed and bound in the UK by BookPrintingUK
Website: www.bookprintinguk.com
YB0589P

FOREWORD

Welcome Reader, to a world of dreams.

For Young Writers' latest competition, we asked our writers to dig deep into their imagination and create a poem that paints a picture of what they dream of, whether it's a make-believe world full of wonder or their aspirations for the future.

The result is this collection of fantastic poetic verse that covers a whole host of different topics. Let your mind fly away with the fairies to explore the sweet joy of candy lands, join in with a game of fantasy football, or you may even catch a glimpse of a unicorn or another mythical creature. Beware though, because even dreamland has dark corners, so you may turn a page and walk into a nightmare!

Whereas the majority of our writers chose to stick to a free verse style, others gave themselves the challenge of other techniques such as acrostics and rhyming couplets.

Each piece in this collection shows the writers' dedication and imagination – we truly believe that seeing their work in print gives them a well-deserved boost of pride, and inspires them to keep writing, so we hope to see more of their work in the future!

CONTENTS

Bibury C Of E Primary School, Cirencester

Cleo Hosken (9)	1
Jennifer Biddle (9)	2
Ava-Rose Lambton Carr (11)	4
Alfred Wenban (9)	5
Iona Inglis (9)	6
Jessica Miles (10)	7
Joshua Drake (8)	8
Violet Baynham (7)	9
Max Cook (8)	10
Poppy Lawrence (9)	11

Birchills CE Community Academy, Walsall

Hashim Akram (9)	12
Masooma Naqvi (9)	14
Kacie Westwood (9)	15
Ameera Imran (8)	16
Ayat Kayani (8)	17
Esmae Bryan (9)	18
Serena Miah (9)	19
Aneesa Jobarteh (8)	20
Roughton Rolland (8)	21

Casterton Sedbergh Preparatory School, Kirkby Lonsdale

Bethany Sapsford (9)	22
Felicity Pelham (8)	24
Madeleine du Cauze de Nazelle (9)	25
Suzie Scott (8)	26
Sam Bentley (8)	27
Harlan King (9)	28

Henry Cavendish (9)	29
Lottie Dinsdale (9)	30
Seb Walker (9)	31
Benjamin Ayling (9)	32
Freddie Robinson (9)	33
Renée Bolton-Price (8)	34
Millie Wills (8)	35
Spencer Oktem (8)	36

Drumduan School, Forres

Erika Lee (11)	37
Louis Reiss (12)	38
Mila Louw (12)	39
Esme Ladaga (12)	40
Caitlin Prendy (12)	41
Chhavi Abhyankar (10)	42
Jonah Sherriff (10)	43
Iris Long (12)	44
Fay Booij (11)	45
Fergus Robertson (11)	46
Ruben Sherriff (10)	47
Joelle Watson (12)	48
Celestee Gibb (12)	49
Lily Smart (11)	50

Eaton House The Manor Girls' School, London

Darcey Payne (8)	51
Georgia Pettigrew (8)	52
Alice Livesey (8)	54
Alice Liu (9)	56
Hars Lu (9)	58
Emma Chang (9)	59
Sahara Latif (9)	60

Eliza Lewellen (8)	61
Arianna Moolwaney (9)	62
Kitty Butler (9)	63
Gabriella Meldrum (9)	64
Ava Skeete-Reid (8)	65

Fallings Park Primary School, Wolverhampton

Emie Crutchley (10)	66
Harper-L'ren Simpson (10)	68
Lexi-Mai Reddell (10)	69
Maddyson Bunsie (11)	70
Diana Nwaigwe (10)	71
Sapphire Moore (11)	72

Fir Ends Primary School, Smithfield

Lewis Corri (10)	73
George Benson (10)	74
Harry Fitton (10)	77
Holly Murray (10)	78
Islay Graham (9)	79
Rosie Hogg (10)	80
Hollie Blair (10)	81
Layla Fox (9)	82
Bodhi Forster (10)	83
Seth Watson (10)	84
Nicky Heugh (10)	85
Tommy Laurie (11)	86
Hattie Poland (10)	87
Max Atkinson (9)	88
Scarlett Graham (9)	89

Hadnall CE Primary School, Hadnall

Beth Thorpe (7)	90
Olivia Jones (8)	91
Maya Beane (7)	92

Kinson Academy, Kinson

Sophie Ferguson (10)	93
Olivia Rose Marsh (10)	94
Joey Pearce (10)	96
Lennie King (10)	98
Nathan (10)	99
Paige Harvey (10)	100
Freya Wells (10)	101
Juliette Sim (8)	102
Skye Morris (9)	103
Amelia Tyrrell (11)	104
Prince Uchegbu (11)	105
Mia Sandever-Lock (10)	106
Maisie Whiffen (8)	107
Ollie Cole (10)	108
Isabella Akanbi (7)	109
Arya Wharton (8)	110
Elsie Shelley (9)	111
Faith Onyinyechukwu (7)	112
Scarlett Bath (8)	113
Lacey-Jane Watson (8)	114
Seth Read (9)	115
Patience Black (8)	116
Isla Bentley (7)	117
Nayana Wright (8)	118
Rio Pearce (8)	119

Our Lady's Catholic Primary School, Latchford

William Wright (9)	120
Daisy Lowther (9)	122
Amellia Jervis (10)	123
Mila Owen (9)	124
Thomas Whewell (10)	125
Kira To (9)	126
Jack Fareham (9)	128
Torin Lam (9)	129
Angelo Amul (9)	130
Holly Woodhouse (10)	131
Zachary Walsh (9)	132
Alice Lee (10)	133
Joel Leicester (10)	134

Sofia Dobson (9)	135

St Elizabeths RC Primary School, Belper

Sienna Pecherska-Brown (10)	136
Erin Clarke (10)	137
Bronte Lawler (10)	138
Mia Groombridge (10)	139
Meredith James (10)	140
Sophie Plastow (11)	141
Alfie Winter (10)	142
Orla Skerritt (10)	143

St John The Baptist CE (VA) Primary School, Pebmarsh

Indie-Rose Cooke (7)	144
Baxter Croton (8)	145
Teddy Andress (8)	146
Lana (9)	147
Ophelia Creamer (8)	148
Arlo Bennet (9)	149
Toby Digby (8)	150
Frank Starckey Gammons (8)	151
Fleur Amos (7)	152
Louis Brown (8)	153
Griff Williamson (8)	154
Olivia Head (8)	155
Finley Smith (9)	156
Edie Short (7)	157
Robyn Porter (8)	158
Saffron Howard (8)	159
Rosie George (8)	160

The Manor CE Primary School, Coalpit Heath

Archie Dykes (10)	161
Anouska King (10)	162
Isaac Beech (11)	164
Ana De Oliveira Calvo (10)	165
Molly Flay (9)	166
Daniel Farr (10)	167

Arthur Parsons (9)	168
Emily Smith (9)	169

Westcourt Primary School, Gravesend

Ruby Imuere (10)	170
Micheline Agyarko (11)	171
Anna-Luisa Souza Garcez (11)	172
Zayn Shiyamin (11)	173
Swettha Vallathan (11)	174
Saaruja Granavel (10)	175
Ayse Koksal (11)	176
Oyinda Soremekun (11)	177
Shayla-Mai Adam (11)	178
Sajjad Madadi (10)	179
Lewis Watson (11)	180
Reggie Jones (11)	181
Aniyah Campbell (11)	182
Charlotte Hatch (11)	183
Klayver Santos Costa (11)	184
Cerys Mannerings (10)	185
Skye Sambrook (11)	186
Tomilola Olusola-Taiwo (10)	187
Lexi Kay (10)	188
Saisha Joshi (10)	189
Deimante Pranskeviciute (11)	190
Jessica Buckland (10)	191
IvyJean Foreman (10)	192
Lilian Nwokorobia (11)	193
Polina Kovalenko (10)	194
Preciouslily Mulvihill (11)	195
Libby Miller (10)	196
Austen Winn-Gordon (10)	197
Stefan Poiana (11)	198
Haaris Samuel (11)	199
Kymami Saddler (10)	200
Imogen Clarke (11)	201
Harry Rose (10)	202
Nimrat Kambaj (11)	203
Jessica Kiskyte (10)	204
Dennis Daukste (11)	205
Guiseppe Forzani (11)	206
Jake Ned (10)	207

Willand School, Willand

Nyra Potts (9)	208
Rosie Luker (9)	209
Rosie Whitehead (9)	210
Holly Isobel James (10)	211

THE POEMS

The Day That My Life Turned Into A Dream

One morning, Max jumped for joy.
Today was the market.
He got dressed and put on his coat,
Walked down the street and sat down on a bench.
He sat there for a second
Then fell into a deep daydream.

In his daydream, he saw...
Flying fairies, writers writing, heroes helping,
Dancing dancing, builders building, teachers teaching,
Workers working, waves waving, lovers loving.

Then he woke up, went home, had dinner,
Went to bed and dreamed about fairies flying,
Writers writing, heroes helping, teachers teaching,
Workers working, waves waving, lovers loving.

Then he woke up and guess what he saw?
Fairies flying, writers writing, heroes helping,
Dancers dancing, builders building, teachers teaching,
Workers working, waves waving, lovers loving.

That day his life turned into a dream.

Cleo Hosken (9)
Bibury C Of E Primary School, Cirencester

On A Rooftop Of Dreams

On a rooftop of dreams,
Under where we all sleep,
Counting all our sheep,
I close my eyes just for a second,
And there I stand on my rooftop of dreams,
With silky, soft clouds by my feet,
There I stare letting go of my cares,
But a frown wipes off my smile on my face,
As there I freeze in horror,
Goblins swoop and loop the loop,
As wolves now look for a new snack to feast on,
I gulp as I see the nightmare King of Terror!

I let out a scream, and I hope destiny will save me,
A whoosh of wings,
A cackle of glee,
But there I lie in a bed of my own,
I let out a sigh of relief leaves my cheeks,
Now everything is not bleak,
You live once, so dream all you can,
Nightmare or not,
Meet me at sunset so we can rejoice,

Hand in hand, never let go,
Build a new path,
Yin and Yang, perfect fit to build a new clan.

Jennifer Biddle (9)
Bibury C Of E Primary School, Cirencester

Once Upon A Where

As I arose in a canopy bed,
My reflection I saw, cheeks are red,
I didn't remember much from the night,
All I knew was that something was not right.

This was not my bed, nor my room,
The sky wandered the gloom, but my sight saw no moon,
The beam in the window blinded my eyes,
Until I could see the bright blue skies.

Trying to get up but something stumped me,
I was wearing a dress and it was not comfy,
Once I got up onto the cold stone floor,
My balance was curved and with that, my toes curled more and more.

I walked up to the window, looking out to the other side,
A sight caught my eye then I slowly sighed,
It was beautiful out there, my brain getting used to it,
A meadow of flowers gracefully growing under a willow tree for a perfect fit.

Ava-Rose Lambton Carr (11)
Bibury C Of E Primary School, Cirencester

In Space

You're in space,
Stars shooting, planets zooming and zipping by,
But there are asteroids pointing your way.

As they pound against the ship, you worry as you dash to the escape pod. Asteroids still pouncing on you like dogs, as you zoom onto an unknown planet.

Crash! You slam into an unknown planet,
And as you climb out, you see bushes, animals,
And trees unlike Earth's.

But then, a dog-like creature runs up to you and rolls over,
As you gently stroke it, you notice its collar says 'Take me to Earth',
You follow the dog, which leads you to a shining space rocket,
And you zoom home.

Alfred Wenban (9)
Bibury C Of E Primary School, Cirencester

Squishmallows

Oh Squishmallows, you bring us delight in our darkest times,
You shine so bright with everything and the smiles we give you.
Squishmallows for life, we couldn't be without you,
Soft and fluffy like clouds, they bring us joy.

They're not just for girls, they could be for boys.
They dance and lie in a moonlit room,
With laughter and not a bit of gloom.
Oh, Squishmallows, oh, Squishmallows I love you so,
Please never leave me, I never want you to go.

Iona Inglis (9)
Bibury C Of E Primary School, Cirencester

A Magical Island

Every night, I get a dream
About something magical.
I went into a fairyland
And saw a pegasus
Flying around then I
Saw a golden deer
In the distance.

I went for a wander and
Saw a cave with a clear
Waterfall falling down
With more pegasus
Inside the cave,
And a golden deer eating
The fresh green grass.

I carried on walking
Through the island
And saw a blue lake.

Jessica Miles (10)
Bibury C Of E Primary School, Cirencester

The Weirdest Dream Ever

In a little brick cottage covered in ivy
And surrounded by trees,
There was a man.
But his house was incredibly messy.
One evening, when the man had tea,
The trees rustled, and the clouds were grey.
He went to bed. He had a dream.
Where his car started to drive itself.
The man chased the car across the world.
But what was driving the car?
It was a cat and a dog.

Joshua Drake (8)
Bibury C Of E Primary School, Cirencester

The Darkness In Your Dreams

When you lay your head down to rest,
You do not think of the scary monsters under the bed,
Monsters are very bad,
They come at night,
They grab you tight,
And they grab you into their den,
So they can hide you,
And as you scream,
They cover your mouth,
You never know if they will let you out!

Violet Baynham (7)
Bibury C Of E Primary School, Cirencester

Pro Spider-Man

He swung into action and beat up all the pro noobs.
Spider-Man is the hero we need to save the world.
He did not see the knife but his spider-sense went off.
And with his spider web, he caught it.
He dropped the knife and fought the bad guy.

Max Cook (8)
Bibury C Of E Primary School, Cirencester

The Cat

The fluff of her fur,
The loving meow,
The proud walk,
The strong growl,
The loving cuddles,
The angry hiss,
The playful heart,
And the happy kiss.

Poppy Lawrence (9)
Bibury C Of E Primary School, Cirencester

Cats With Kittens

I could see a land
Full of cats,
I could see the cats
Were on mats.

I was somewhere
With cats and kittens,
The cats were in baths
And the kittens were in mittens.

I was with someone
Called my mother,
I was with my mother
But also my brothers.

I felt very chill,
Because the cats
Put on a kitten film.

The cats
Gave me some cuddles,
And for the kittens
I blew some bubbles.

After the movie,
We drank
Strawberry smoothies.

The cats
Were black and white,
Their fur was soft
And also light.

Hashim Akram (9)
Birchills CE Community Academy, Walsall

Untitled

It was a scary night.
I was in a dark forest.
I was terrified! Terrified!
When out came a scary wizard,
Who said, "I'll be your guide!"
The moon shimmered on his robe.
As he whispered quietly.
"Ala' kasam!" he boomed.
Then a portal came up, shining brightly.
He said, "Come in, come in!"
I entered in as a loud noise said,
"Hurry! Hurry up!"
Then with a blinding flash,
I saw my house.

Masooma Naqvi (9)
Birchills CE Community Academy, Walsall

The Significant Athlete

I could see an athlete swinging on the bars,
She went so high she could have been on Mars,
Then as she slipped on her wrist,
Everyone started to panic,
It was a little bit dramatic,

As she stood up, she shook it off,
She was such a show off!
Her last routine was the beam,
And it was such a dream,

She tried to do a handstand,
And ended up in a headstand,
It was a very disastrous day.

Kacie Westwood (9)
Birchills CE Community Academy, Walsall

A Tale Of Friendship And Fire

Colours of the rainbow,
Shining so bright,
Me and my unicorn,
Flying in the soft sunlight.

But here comes a dragon, big and bold,
With fiery breath, so fierce and cold,
Castles crumble, palaces fall,
The buildings are no longer tall.

Dragon roared but we were strong,
Trying to destroy him took way too long,
In the end we won the day,
Me and my unicorn, hooray!

Ameera Imran (8)
Birchills CE Community Academy, Walsall

My Weird Dream!

I meet my favourite dinosaur, called a tyrannosaurus rex,
I'm surrounded by strange people,
These people go to the steeple,
I'm in a strange, creepy cave,
Where people gave,
I feel as scared as can be,
These people are weird, I can see,
This dinosaur sees and I run as fast as I can,
Until I see a man,
I've ended up on a TV show,
Uh oh!

Ayat Kayani (8)
Birchills CE Community Academy, Walsall

The Dancer

I met an artist,
Now my days
Are printed in lavender,
Every hour a different hue.

I dream in watercolour,
Dance in coloured tones,
With each stroke I glide,
Moved by inspiration.

I am his vision, his dancer,
His impression of beauty.
This canvas, my stage,
As I perform for you.

Esmae Bryan (9)
Birchills CE Community Academy, Walsall

Wizarding World

Once upon a dream was a wizarding world,
Where potions and spells make the bells chime to tell people the time,
In a tree is a dog called Lime,
Go across the tree house bridge,
To the potion room, where a potion lies in a cauldron brewing,
A queasy feeling hits,
The potion disappears,
And a book appears.

Serena Miah (9)
Birchills CE Community Academy, Walsall

The Clown With The Forest

The clown is a thing,
It cackles and tackles,
Until everyone gets away,
It all starts with a clown,
That all starts with a tackle,
It's scary there, it's dark there,
Once you see a clown,
You'd better run!

Aneesa Jobarteh (8)
Birchills CE Community Academy, Walsall

The Darkness

Trees, trees, trees all around me,
The breeze, breeze, breeze swishing past me.
All this darkness, all around me,
Makes me more scared than I should be.
When sunshine comes, I'll be happy,
Until darkness, oh no!

Roughton Rolland (8)
Birchills CE Community Academy, Walsall

My Space Owl And I

My owl's feathers are the colour of moonlight,
I feel exhilarated as we take flight.

Swooping, soaring way up high,
My mystical owl flaps through the sky.

First, we will visit the sun,
Solar system here I come.

Mercury is pretty tiny,
Up in space, no one can find me.

Over there is red-hot Venus,
I hope the satellite has not seen us!

Earth is next with land and seas,
The only planet with plants and trees.

My owl's wings flap, I feel the thrust,
While rocky Mars is covered in dust.

Gas giant Jupiter's shadow looms,
Around it orbit lots of moons.

Magnificent rings encircle Saturn,
Rock and ice form a stripy pattern.

My owl swoops around Uranus, spinning on its side,
What an amazing sight this is, my eyes are open wide.

Neptune is the planet of storms and cold,
Luckily I'm wearing my warm gown of gold.

Now our journey must end, home we must fly,
Back to Earth, back to bed, my space owl and I.

Bethany Sapsford (9)
Casterton Sedbergh Preparatory School, Kirkby Lonsdale

Black Castle

I wake up to see I am in a forest,
I turn around to see I am not in a forest,
But I need a tourist.
A giant black castle right in front of me.
I turn to Renee and she can clearly see
That giant black castle towering over us.
What am I saying? I am such a mess.
But where is Lottie?
There she is, in that window, good spotting.
Oh no, she is in a cage!
I have to help her go back on stage.
Me and Renee go inside the castle.
Even if we're scared, we have to battle.
We climb up the stairs
And hide behind a wall.
People shouting then Lottie starts to fall!
I run down the stairs and jump on.

Felicity Pelham (8)
Casterton Sedbergh Preparatory School, Kirkby Lonsdale

The Dark And Light World

In the dark and light world
Light Tinker Bell twirled.
With her magical dust that looks like stars
While the beast stands there with his scars.

Scary as can be
I bet people on Earth would not laugh at me.
Oh, all the monsters I hate
A unicorn asks, "Do you want a ride, mate?"

Of course I said yes
But that made a mess.
The unicorn was bad
Unlike a good lad
The monster unicorn was flying me to a haunted castle
For a big battle
It looked scary
With a monster very hairy
I tried to stop the fight.

Madeleine du Cauze de Nazelle (9)
Casterton Sedbergh Preparatory School, Kirkby Lonsdale

My Dragons

Dragons are majestic and magic,
So I decided to get one in my dream.
I asked a wizard to conjure some up,
And these are their names.

Maroon the Mud Dragon,
A real ankle-biter.
Violet the Echo Dragon,
A really good fighter.

Velda the Bone Dragon,
All winter white.
And Nether the Fire Dragon,
He has a fiery temper.

Aqua the Water Dragon,
A really good swimmer.
Makes the Air Dragon,
A very swift flyer.

So I think they are enough for now.

Suzie Scott (8)
Casterton Sedbergh Preparatory School, Kirkby Lonsdale

Snakes In The Night

Camouflaged even inside your bedroom
On your peg, even on your shoe
But most of all in the jungle.

You do not see them until it's too late
Slithering in the woods, unnoticeable or so you think
In a flash of a blink, it is the last you see.

But it's not their fault they're so scary,
Their key is to catch rodents, leave them alone
And you will be rewarded with nature's pest control.

Sam Bentley (8)
Casterton Sedbergh Preparatory School, Kirkby Lonsdale

Evil Dreams

E agles come and pull me down,
V ultures come and eat me up,
I nnocent people find their death,
L onely monsters come and sweat.

D eadly spiders, snakes and more,
R evolting rats,
E at and eat until they're full,
A nts come and eat the rest,
M icroscopic bits are left,
S tuck in darkness, day into night.

Harlan King (9)
Casterton Sedbergh Preparatory School, Kirkby Lonsdale

Lonely Void

D reams are
R eally mysterious. I am in a dark void. I
E nter a black hole with the help of my dragon
A nd me and
M y mighty dragon
W ander about the new worlds. And for
O ne moment I feel free
R oaming around, just me
L onely is not as bad as you see
D rifting away, being set free.

Henry Cavendish (9)
Casterton Sedbergh Preparatory School, Kirkby Lonsdale

Unicorn Universe

D aring is how I feel,
R iding through a waterfall,
E verything is beautiful!
A t once I see some... wait!
M y eyes must be deceiving me!
L ooking closer I can see
A unicorn, my horse and me,
N ow I am flying fast and free!
D azzling colours fly around me.

Lottie Dinsdale (9)
Casterton Sedbergh Preparatory School, Kirkby Lonsdale

Bog Dog

I am a three-headed dog
And I live in a bog
I love to be muddy and wet
And I do not want to be a pet

I live in Monster Land
With lots of sucking quicksand
Land is short and food is slow
I am a predator
Always on the go

If I appear in your dreams
You will scream!

Seb Walker (9)
Casterton Sedbergh Preparatory School, Kirkby Lonsdale

Timmy The Magic Turtle

Waking up on a desert island,
I see a man selling a magic turtle,
Timmy is green with yellow stripes,
He gets into lots of fights,
Dueling with fearless force,
Turtles chant Timmy's name,
He is the bravest turtle I know,
His belly is big; he likes to eat.

Benjamin Ayling (9)
Casterton Sedbergh Preparatory School, Kirkby Lonsdale

Midnight Monsters

M ega greedy like pigs,
O wls hoot like a car horn,
N asty, I am like jellyfish,
S harp claws like knives,
T errible squeals like mice,
E ar screeching screams pierce the night,
R apid like cheetahs,
S cary!

Freddie Robinson (9)
Casterton Sedbergh Preparatory School, Kirkby Lonsdale

The Brilliant Dancer

I am a dancer
In a white flowing dress
I leap like a leopard
And balance like a flamingo
I feel excited and alive
Dancing with my friends
Parents are watching
Proud as peacocks
Smiling wide smiles
Like The Cheshire Cat.

Renée Bolton-Price (8)
Casterton Sedbergh Preparatory School, Kirkby Lonsdale

Red Carpet

F eeling free
A dele looks bewitching
M arvellous people, are they?
O n the ruby-red carpet
U nder the moonlit stage
S urprisingly, I hear my name
But it's just my mum
What a shame.

Millie Wills (8)
Casterton Sedbergh Preparatory School, Kirkby Lonsdale

Night Fright

A monster stands in front of me,
I don't recognise anything I see,
Trees are blood red,
Skulls are asleep in bed,
I hear deadly screams,
Luckily, it is just my dream.

Spencer Oktem (8)
Casterton Sedbergh Preparatory School, Kirkby Lonsdale

Dreams And Nightmares

Dreams about dogs and dreams about cats.
Dreams about frogs and dreams about bats.
Dreams always come and dreams always go!
Nightmares come and nightmares go.
Dream about swinging on a swing.
Dream about talking or always singing.
Dream about rocking to and fro,
Dream about playing rock and roll!
Dream about brothers who are singing!
Dream about sisters who are always prancing!
Dream about going on magical missions!
Or, dream about bus and train stations.
But, sometimes nightmares give us a scare,
Like tumbling down on steep, big stairs.
Or, falling into a deep, deep well!
More or less trapped in a shell.
Nightmares that tell you your teacher's gone mad!
Or, nightmares that tell you the future is bad!
Nightmares always give us a fright,
But always dream and sleep tight!

Erika Lee (11)
Drumduan School, Forres

Untitled

Time ticks on through the whole wide world
Through humans, through plants, through animals curled
Through rocks, through water, through stars and through birds
And why am I here? This place is absurd
This city is smoky through day and through night
I dream of a place where nature is in sight
But where should I go - to the left or the right?
To go there, is it easy or is it a plight?
I dream that I sail in a very large ocean
The waves guide me slowly in a beautiful motion
The water is as if it was the earth's lotion
That land I dream of would be my devotion
But what would it look like that land of mine?
And would there be oak, or would there be pine?
And would... Oh dear, it's half past nine.

Louis Reiss (12)
Drumduan School, Forres

My Nightly Adventures

One night I lie in bed,
Wondering when it will be,
When my imagination carries me away,
Away to the land of dreams!

All of a sudden, my room starts to shake,
Something's so awfully loud,
And in through the window zooms,
A little, tiny cloud.

It beckons to me, I get on its back,
We fly away over the moon,
Through the clouds and past the stars,
In the nightly gloom.

A light comes from the east,
The sky is painted gold.
I look and stare at the glowing sky,
It's a great sight to behold!

But then the image fades away,
There's no more to be seen,
Again, I'm lying in my bed,
Thinking of my dream!

Mila Louw (12)
Drumduan School, Forres

Dreamland

N ighttime is approaching, I'm scared to enter Dreamland
I close my eyes and hope for water or sand!
G oblins, ogres, trolls all around, fun at me they poke
H ere! The dark enfolds me in their cloak
T he beautiful land! Alas! I now wrinkle my nose at the smell
M any's the time I've been here, I remember it well
A lthough I am terrified, I somehow begin to flee
R *oar!* I stumble and suddenly darkness is all I see
E ventually, I awake and have no trouble coming to the conclusion that sleep is overrated.

Esme Ladaga (12)
Drumduan School, Forres

Monsters!

N ow it is night-time as I fall asleep in my bed.
I dream about ickabogs, dragons and ghouls in my shed.
G oblins and gremlins, they creep up my stairs.
H ere in my bed, I try to say my prayers.
T he darkness is creeping, my parents still sleeping.
M y eyes open as before, they creep up to the door.
A s I look up and get a fright, my mum comes and asks, "Alright?"
R iley, my friend, walks through the door.
E ventually, I am not scared anymore.

Caitlin Prendy (12)
Drumduan School, Forres

My Weird Dream

Daffodils white and daffodils blue,
They can be seen from a mile or two,
Depends if they are made from glue,
Or if you want them brand new.

But one stands out just like you,
Do you know? Shall I give you a clue?
Are you ready? Could this be true?
Why don't you think it through?

The rest of my dream was put in a stew,
And all that was left was but a few,
Suddenly I woke up in my bed,
Thinking of the weird dream in my head.

Chhavi Abhyankar (10)
Drumduan School, Forres

Nightmares

N ights are dark and cold, when I lie in bed,
I dream about monsters, I dream about ghouls while
G hostly shadows are creeping around,
H igh and low, not making a sound.
T ime's running out and I can't move.
M ad thoughts are forming in the back of my head,
A m I alive or am I dead?
R olling over in my bed,
E vil thoughts are in me deep
S omehow ending my endless sleep.

Jonah Sherriff (10)
Drumduan School, Forres

Creepy Corners

N ighttime horror in my head
I am lying in my bed
G rowling noises are all around
H ide under the covers, quick!
T hen something grabs my foot, is this a trick?
M any monsters I see, all of them so hairy!
A *rgh!* I'm pulled down, down, down
R eality comes crashing around and I open my eyes
E ventually, my breathing calms and I keep telling myself it was all just a nightmare.

Iris Long (12)
Drumduan School, Forres

Nightmare

N othing could prepare me for such a night,
I am surrounded by a horrible sight,
G oblins, dragons and werewolves too,
H ere and there I hear a *boo!*
T rolls and ogres fill me with dread,
M y head is spinning, am I dead?
A my my friend has turned into a beast,
R iding towards her human feast,
E ating children in her lair,
S uddenly I wake up, it was just a nightmare.

Fay Booij (11)
Drumduan School, Forres

Nightmare

N ightmares, oh so bad they can be!
I prefer the happy dreams like
G reen grass in the meadow, not a sad sight to see or a
H en wearing a helmet as happy as can be or
T he great Fergus sitting on his throne but to think
M e a king, as royal as can be or an
A stronaut jumping on the moon but I
R ealise I am not asleep so I close my eyes and
E nter slowly the nightly portal of sleep.

Fergus Robertson (11)
Drumduan School, Forres

Nightmares

My dreams are often nightmares,
They guide me throughout the night,
They often bring me back in time,
And then I start to fight.

Orks and dragons roar out loud,
Fire breath and black storm clouds,
I fight and fight, my head is spinning,
Then someone tells me it's only the beginning.

I wake up cold with sweat,
In my bed at home,
And I am very glad,
My nightmares have now gone.

Ruben Sherriff (10)
Drumduan School, Forres

Dream Of Snow

Snow falls softly all around,
Nightly figures of the ground,
On they go round and round,
Whirling, curling with a bound,

On they go then come the hound,
No more joy to be found!
Suddenly, it's all so sound,
None can hear the silent pound,

Snow falls softly all around,
Nightly figures of the ground,
On they go round and round,
Whirling, curling with a bound.

Joelle Watson (12)
Drumduan School, Forres

The Snow

D eep in my sleep, I dream of snow,
R olling and whirling with a glow,
E ach snowflake has a beautiful pattern; they fall in a flow,
A fter a while, the snow gets thin and slow,
M oving forward, I see a beautiful doe,
S uddenly, I woke up in my room, my hair covered with snow.

Celestee Gibb (12)
Drumduan School, Forres

Flying Chicks

Twenty-five fluffy chicks fall off a rainbow,
Fly to space and find another rainbow,
In space and they sit on it, and fall off it,
They wake up to realise it was just a dream,
And they are still on this little rainbow.

Lily Smart (11)
Drumduan School, Forres

The Night My Toys Came Alive

As soon as I turned off my light,
My dreams swirled in the night,
Alive came my friendly toys,
They were old, they were young,
They were girls and boys.
My toys, my toys, they were alive!

I followed them through a door,
Onto a moor,
Were they taking me to a magical land?
I thought this was a moor, but there was so much sand,
Away I went, away I went, with my toys.

Oh, this land I did see,
It was such a sight in front of me.
There was a toy house,
Even a clockwork mouse,
This land of toys, it was such a sight,
I didn't want to leave, however, I might.

Darcey Payne (8)
Eaton House The Manor Girls' School, London

The Flightmare

Tucked up in my bed
All cosy and tight,
I put down my head
All ready for night.

The pillow so soft
I'm ready for sleep,
But now I'm aloft -
I'm too scared to peep!

It feels like I'm falling
Right through the sky,
The birds are all cawing
And clouds whizzing by.

I'm very high up
And hold myself tight,
To make sure my teddies
Don't fall through the night.

I call out for help
But no one replies,
Is anyone out there
Or only the skies?

I'm spinning and falling
My fear grows and grows,
It feels like it's real
But nobody knows.

Off in the distance
A pink fluffy cloud,
I aim with persistence -
Am I calling out loud?

I land with a thump
In a candyfloss world,
In my throat is a lump
My body still curled.

The sun hits my eyes
My teddies are there,
By the night flies -
I'm back in my lair.

The slightest of beams
Makes me wake with a start,
Although with my dreams
It's a sadness to part.

Georgia Pettigrew (8)
Eaton House The Manor Girls' School, London

My Excellent And Amazing World Of Dreams

In the deep, dark depths
Of a mysterious cave,
There lives an old troll
As small as a mole.

He's got warts,
He's got spots,
He's covered in
Bright pink polka dots!

There are blue and green stripes
Running down his back,
And his eyes are mystical,
Big and black.

Not far away,
On a very tall hill,
There dwells a dragon
By the name of Phil.

He's scary, he's mean!
He's an absolute tyrant!
And his ways, oh dear,
They're so grumpy and violent!

With smoke leaking out
Of his nose and ears,
With just one sight of him,
You'll burst into tears!

Now up, up we go
To the cliffs of ice and snow,
Where fairies and pixies
Have always been foes.

They've had fights, they've had wars,
It was a horrible phase.
After all that battling,
They live in opposite ways.

It's way more magical
Than it seems,
My excellent and amazing
World of dreams.

Alice Livesey (8)
Eaton House The Manor Girls' School, London

Dream Land

I was feeling so exasperated,
That I fell asleep in bed.
I thought I heard a voice,
"Who are you?" someone said.

I woke up discombobulated,
And I saw a unicorn.
With a pulchritudinous mane,
And a sparkly horn.

I couldn't believe my eyes,
And wondered who was speaking.
But all I found was the unicorn,
And surprised myself by shrieking!

Once I became calm again,
I divulged to her my name.
Then the unicorn replied,
"Oh, I have the same!"

"Where are we, Sophie?"
I then queried.
She said, "Dream Land."
"Oh no, Mum will be worried!"

"I'll fly you home,
Have no fear.
Jump on my back,
And you can steer."

Suddenly the unicorn hit a bump,
I landed in bed.
I heard Mum say,
"Wake up, we are going to the bay!"

Alice Liu (9)
Eaton House The Manor Girls' School, London

The Fantastic Dream

I dreamt that Miss Marianna came to my tenth birthday party.
We ate delicious cake and drank lots of Chinese green tea.
I dreamt that I became a famous fashion designer,
And became Miss Marianna's wedding dress signer.
I dreamt that I became a talented artist,
And my work was displayed in Buckingham Palace.
I dreamt that I won a Nobel Prize,
For finding a new species with magnificent eyes.
I dreamt that I walked on the red carpet,
And everyone ran to the fashion market.
I dreamt that I drank a special potion,
Which made me fly, and gave me motion.

Hars Lu (9)
Eaton House The Manor Girls' School, London

I Was In Space

There were stars surrounding me
And did they ask me for tea?
Oh dear, oh dear, this was so strange
Was this a bed? Oh what a change!

I was floating, it felt like flying
And the sun was shining
There was a black hole
I could do an entire roll.

The sun was so bright
I felt very light
The stars were winking
And even tinkling.

I landed on the moon
What was the time? It felt like noon!
I jumped so high
I loved to fly!

Emma Chang (9)
Eaton House The Manor Girls' School, London

The Magnificent Castle

When I close my eyes and sleep,
I enter a magical land.

Full of rolling emerald hills,
And cloudless blue skies,
Where sheep graze happily,
And butterflies flutter from leaf to leaf.

I walk straight toward a magnificent castle,
It stands up tall, strong and sturdy,
It is golden and gleaming,
Shiny and glittering.

I smile in my sleep,
As I step into the magnificent castle.

Sahara Latif (9)
Eaton House The Manor Girls' School, London

My Magnificent Meal!

There was a meal under a tray,
I lifted it up and,
The peas went astray,
They danced, they pranced,
And ended up on the floor!

The fantastic, flipping fish started to snicker,
From the broccoli bouncing up and down.
The hot potatoes were all a flicker,
As the parsley twirled and whirled around.
The moping mop took a breath,
Before cleaning it up!

Eliza Lewellen (8)
Eaton House The Manor Girls' School, London

Space, Space

I want to float in space
And take part in a race.
Go floating in the sky
No time to eat pie.

Land on the moon
Better not take a spoon.
Go to Venus and Mars
To go soar with the stars.

To listen to silence
But I need a licence.
To drink orange juice
Not let the air pipe loose.

Arianna Moolwaney (9)
Eaton House The Manor Girls' School, London

My Magic Flower

I had a magic flower, it was very small,
A few minutes later it was very tall!
I climbed and climbed to the top,
And I found out it could hop!
It can walk, talk and even blink,
When I came close to it, we just had a link.
So when I saw this power,
It was me and my magic flower.

Kitty Butler (9)
Eaton House The Manor Girls' School, London

The Day The Chickens Took Over

In October,
The chickens took over,
A whole fleet arrived,
We were all surprised,
First, they started marching,
Then they started charging,
Squawking and running,
They were quite cunning,
And soon they took over
All of Dover!

Gabriella Meldrum (9)
Eaton House The Manor Girls' School, London

Raven Chase

I was a raven, chasing Dad,
Seeing who was the winner, really quite mad.
I jumped upon walls, he jumped upon trees,
But we always jumped in threes.
One, two, three,
One, two, *whee!*
Oh, the fun I had,
Raven - chasing with Dad.

Ava Skeete-Reid (8)
Eaton House The Manor Girls' School, London

Dinosaur

The rustle of the leaves;
From the ground to the trees,
You can't escape its powerful bite,
As it stalks its prey into the night.
With bone-breaking teeth,
And blood-dripping jaw,
You'll quiver when you hear its roar.
He's coming for us all!

My heart is racing, for he is chasing,
For he is roaring, never snoring.
He is gruesome and appalling, he is not meant for ignoring.
In the night, he is stirring fright,
With colossal teeth and a mammoth jaw,
Your heart will be thumping when you hear its roar.

This beast is overloaded with thrill, as it has caught its final kill.
As he hides in the night, his teeth shine bright.
But sooner or later, it'll catch its bite.
Then it hides back into the night, causing nothing but fright.

You'll quiver with fear when you see its sight,
Nothing but fear, nothing but fright.
As it is normally dug out the sand,
The museum where it's located is very grand.
As we find them in Loch Ness, as we thought they were dead,
They could possibly be under our beds!
As they were once fossils, these dinos are colossal.

Our history teachers have lied, there's nowhere left to hide,
These dinosaurs should've died.

Emie Crutchley (10)
Fallings Park Primary School, Wolverhampton

At Grass!

My heart is pumping, I'm in an arena.
My white-coated horse is in its stable drinking.
I'm worried as everyone hops on their horses.
One... Two... Three... *Go!*
Everyone is leaping bar over bar
I'm behind Buttercup.
"Faster, faster," I'm saying.
All of a sudden, it's working
I'm in front of everyone
Galloping around the arena
I'm so close to the finish
As everyone in the crowd is screaming,
"Go, Harper, go!"
I'm panting as I dive over the finish line
"Woo! Yes, Harper!"
I get off my horse as everyone congratulates me.
I'm getting given this gold trophy
I hold it up, jumping up and down
And screaming in happiness!
Bye for now.

Harper-L'ren Simpson (10)
Fallings Park Primary School, Wolverhampton

Mythical Creatures

M y dreams take me away at night,
Y et this land is too bright.
T ake me away to a mythical land,
H elp me and give a hand.
I want to go to the realm of dragons,
C ould I ride on the floating wagons?
A lso in the realm of monsters,
L ies a group of flying lobsters.

C reative creatures fly across the sky,
R ight, left, right, left, I can't say bye.
E ven though I will let out a moan,
A ll I have to do is go home.
T omorrow I will return,
U nlike bringing a ribbon,
R emember me,
E nter the sea,
S o you can find the hidden treasure!

Lexi-Mai Reddell (10)
Fallings Park Primary School, Wolverhampton

Fashion Designer

F antastic clothing gets made every day,
A nd makes joy in the world,
S ome may be expensive,
H owever, they can be cheap.
I ncredible people desire to be a fashion designer,
O nly you can design which styles you like,
N ot everyone likes threads and fabrics, but you choose your own path.

D on't ever doubt yourself,
E ven if you don't get it first try,
S ince you are human, you make mistakes,
I f you proceed to make clothing,
G reat things will happen,
N ever give up,
E veryone needs time.
R ight things happen for a reason.

Maddyson Bunsie (11)
Fallings Park Primary School, Wolverhampton

The Awakening Of A Fairy Tale

I looked up and to my surprise
A figure in a disguise
Roamed around a fairy town
To see the wonders of joy
A glimpse of something made him frown
The sight of a wonderful baby boy
Witches and wizards
Fairies and warlocks
Gathered around to see the sight of the creature
It wasn't a boy and it wasn't a girl
But no one could see the hiding figure
For all this time he was under a bleacher
I felt so dizzy everything was a blur
Suddenly my brain had a transfer
I was in my bed like a human being
Was I dreaming?
Who knows?

Diana Nwaigwe (10)
Fallings Park Primary School, Wolverhampton

My Fairy Adventure

Fairies here, fairies there
Their sparkling wings are everywhere
Flying low, flying high
Flying high so I can reach the sky.

Toadstool houses on the hills
Not far from the windmills
Now over there
Now over here.

They ask me to come on a fairy adventure
Now so high I can almost reach the sky
I ask if they will come back
Maybe we will see.

Sapphire Moore (11)
Fallings Park Primary School, Wolverhampton

A Football Fantasy

In my dream one night,
I have to hold onto the goalpost tight,
And in the stadium light,
I see George practising his tricks,
Vollies and bicycle kicks,
Here comes a mystery person,
Who could it be?
Is it a case of an unsolved mystery?
Here comes Luca with a mischievous grin,
He comes out and volleys it into the bin,
Here comes Michael to the penalty spot,
Here he comes for the kick, almost over the crossbar,
But in the top bin it goes,
To the halfway line, I go
And volley it over away,
It goes towards the goal line,
It flies wide,
And the ball creeps over the goal line,
Like a bowling ball,
Strike at the dead of night.
Out comes the sun, it's time to go home.

Lewis Corri (10)
Fir Ends Primary School, Smithfield

My Football Dream

As I drifted off into my dream,
Will it be as it seems?
I was flying into the stadium,
I was wondering if it was made of titanium
As I saw Mbappé run onto the field
I saw a security guard holding a shield,
I tied my football laces around my ankles tight,
I could see the sun shining very bright
As I got ready to run onto the pitch,
I really hoped that I didn't have a stitch,
In the distance, I saw Messi doing tricks,
While Ronaldo was practising his bicycle kicks,
I ran onto the football pitch, to see daylight,
Then I saw some goalkeepers who were some height,
As the match was about to begin, I got prepared,
In the distance, I saw a goalkeeper with a big glare,
As the match started to begin, I started to run really fast,
I was hoping I wouldn't let out any gas,
Then we started to score, one, two, three and four,
I was wondering if we could score any more,
Then I started to do more cool tricks,
Then I got the confidence to do some bicycle kicks,

Five, six, seven, eight,
Since we were beating them, why not go and celebrate?
The halftime whistle was coming quick and fast,
I shouldn't have eaten those beans, because there's going to be... gas,
The halftime whistle had gone fast
I might as well say gracias,
The fifteen-minute break will be good too
Because I will have time to go to the loo,
Then the second half started to begin,
We had a big chance, we would win,
I suddenly got goosebumps left and right,
I hoped I didn't lose my appetite,
Nine, ten, eleven, twelve,
Now I thought the other team would rebel,
Now I was getting tired and kinda had a stitch,
I didn't know if I could do another bicycle kick,
Six minutes was coming really fast,
I thought I might let out an enormous gas,
Neymar Jr came out onto the pitch,
Wow, he was doing some really cool tricks,
The fulltime whistle was coming fast,
Will I be able to say gracias?
Moments later, I saw the clock,

Ninety minutes was on, will I lose the plot?
When the referee blew the whistle fast,
I still got to say gracias.

George Benson (10)
Fir Ends Primary School, Smithfield

Strange Dreams

S tarlight shines in the night sky
T winkling dots up so high
R ound my bed, the cat seems to fly
A s a golem-like creature runs on by
N ow is where things get strange
G liding in a moonlit cave
E verything starts to wobble and wave

D ragons fly all around
R iding a dragon feels so free when you're not hitting the ground
E lephants munch on meat but keep their plates nice and neat
A kraken tries to grab me but he's put back by a big green sheet
M y eyes seem to flutter and a distant voice calls me
S o goodbye for now and then it was over, without a sound.

Harry Fitton (10)
Fir Ends Primary School, Smithfield

My Dream Land

In a jar full of sparks, my dream whizzes,
And it flops me up, it flops me down,
It sends me into a magical land,
A whole bundle of fun has just begun!

Multicoloured aliens fly over my head,
Unicorns pull my beautiful bed,
Fairies glide, now down a gigantic slide,
Into the chocolate factory, I glide.

A chocolatey gaze but I'm not fazed,
A guy in a red cloak drinking coke,
The hover chocolate I eat,
The air begins under my feet,
Another flop, another round,
Back into my bed, safe and sound.

Holly Murray (10)
Fir Ends Primary School, Smithfield

The Underwater Elements

Underwater in the clouds,
There were mermaids making sounds,
While in the cave, the merhorses gazed,
Into the aqua-green crystal cave,
On a carpet of white waves.

A clamshell with crystal white pearls, they played,
There were water doves bobbing beneath the waves,
Oh, the way that they behaved,
Among the sea shells and the waves.

In the palace far beyond,
There was a merhorse with his magic horn,
Beyond the ocean floor, the crystal palace gleamed,
That's what's in my dreams.

Islay Graham (9)
Fir Ends Primary School, Smithfield

Pirate Ship Peril

I was never prepared to wake like this,
Bound and tied on a pirate ship!
Oh no! Oh dear, my biggest fear,
Blackbeard the pirate suddenly appears!

As he rips off the tape, he lays my fate.
To be thrown into the sea!
Oh heck, oh dearie me, I'm about to become history!

As I'm dragged onto the deck,
I become wet with sweat.
At last will my watery end be met?

At last I'm thrown down to drown,
Then I wake, draped in my dressing gown!

Rosie Hogg (10)
Fir Ends Primary School, Smithfield

The Best Dream Ever

As I sleep in my comfy bed,
Broomsticks fly around in my head,
Potions, spells and the strangest smells,
The Harry Potter tales JK tells.

I am transported to Hogwarts, wow!
I am playing a game of quidditch now.
I am all sweating, now time for a bath,
No, there's Moaning Myrtle, she's on the roof,
Sneaking up to scare me.

A boo and a few, it's the end,
Of my Hogwarts trip now.

Hollie Blair (10)
Fir Ends Primary School, Smithfield

The Unicorn

In my dreams,
Every night,
Upon the clouds,
Wondering how I saw
A shimmering unicorn,
With a single horn,
I hopped up on its glowing back,
And galloped to the magic sea.
I whispered,
"How could this be?"
When it stopped,
Off I hopped,
I wondered if this was a trap,
I looked around to find a map,
I swam towards the deep blue sea,
I saw a palace there for me!

Layla Fox (9)
Fir Ends Primary School, Smithfield

Football

As I dream upon my bed,
thoughts of football fill my head.
Man United, Carlisle too,
my favourite teams to name a few.
Rashford, Garnacho, Højlund and Fernandes,
I could go on but the list is endless.
Onto the football pitch I run,
luckily the match has just begun.
I shoot, I score, the crowd makes a deafening roar, the commentator yells,
"Forster scores!"

Bodhi Forster (10)
Fir Ends Primary School, Smithfield

The Caves

Dreams, dreams, dreams,
Light slowly fades
Darker than the murky sky and the deep dark caves
Down into the centre of the Earth I fall
Trying to find my way back I crawl
Through the wet and slimy ground
What is that? What have I found?
Could this be my way home?
Here is a patch, well known
I speedily run as fast as I can
And into my bed and back awake
I slam!

Seth Watson (10)
Fir Ends Primary School, Smithfield

Cookie Dreams

I slept upon my comfy bed,
Thoughts of puddings in my head.

Chocolate cookies, gingerbread people,
Pancakes drip with syrup and treacle.
A portal made of chocolate gold,
In my hand, cake swords I hold.

Hungry monsters I must kill,
Before I eat so much I'm ill,
The brownie overlord, I must defeat,
But all around, I want to eat.

Nicky Heugh (10)
Fir Ends Primary School, Smithfield

The Ground

I looked down upon a cloud,
Jumped from a plane, screaming loud,
I was floating down towards the ground,
Nothing but the air all around,
Suddenly, I hit the ground,
And heard an odd sound,
It was me hitting the rock-hard floor.

Tommy Laurie (11)
Fir Ends Primary School, Smithfield

Football Dream

Once upon a football dream
I signed for Man U, my favourite team!

My football strip as red as blood
To all that doubted I said I could!

Now off to continue my football dream
I now signed for the Man City team!

Hattie Poland (10)
Fir Ends Primary School, Smithfield

The Land

In a dusty land far far away
This is where my dreams take me every day
With a crash and a bang and I'm here
Oh dear, my greatest fear
A monstrous deer
But there I lie awake in bed.

Max Atkinson (9)
Fir Ends Primary School, Smithfield

Up Above

Once upon a white, fluffy cloud,
Saphire skies and birds so loud,
Running fast along the sky,
Crystal clouds rushing by.

Scarlett Graham (9)
Fir Ends Primary School, Smithfield

Wizards And Monsters

A wizard wanders through a wood,
Trying to cast a spell.
Out flies a dragon breathing flames,
And down the wizard fell.

The monsters are hatching a cunning plan,
To take the wizard's wand.
Smoke, ash and fire fill the air,
They don't think it will take long.

But the wizard knows what's going on,
He knows how to escape.
With an alakazam the monsters fade,
The dragon flies off at speed.

Because they've taken on Harry Potter
Who is a very good wizard indeed.

Beth Thorpe (7)
Hadnall CE Primary School, Hadnall

A Wonderful Dream

When I close my eyes at night,
I hope to dream about this wonderful sight,
Where flowers blossom, and trees are grown,
And every person on Earth has a home,
There would be no fighting,
Just peace allowed,
Singing and joy amongst the crowd,
When I close my eyes at night,
I hope to dream about this wonderful sight.

Olivia Jones (8)
Hadnall CE Primary School, Hadnall

Dream Kittens

K ittens play in the dead of night,
I see them dance in the moonlight,
T hey are so lively, so full of fun,
T omorrow they'll snooze in the warm, hot sun.
E very time I cannot sleep, cats I count,
N ot fluffy sheep.
S o now I close my eyes to rest, fluffy kittens are the best.

Maya Beane (7)
Hadnall CE Primary School, Hadnall

Dream About Peace

I dream of a life of peace
Wherein I can live a life of ease
Where there's no difference in being black or white
And everyone can walk the street anytime at night.

I dream of a life of happiness
No room for hate and selfishness
Equality for all, doesn't matter if one's rich or poor
Acknowledging the greatness that lies at our core.

I dream of life's existence with
No room for hate and selfishness
Women and men need equal rights
Instead of all these horrifying fights!

I dream of a life of serenity and kindness
Where we can all understand the value of love is priceless
To be different and it's okay and discrimination doesn't kill.
Loving ourselves, each other and doing God's will would be the best deal!

Sophie Ferguson (10)
Kinson Academy, Kinson

My Dream

M y dream is to be a gymnast or footballer,
Y ou should never give up on any dream - make it come true.

D etermined, I always am,
R emember nothing is impossible, it's just in your mind,
E veryone watching as I achieve it,
A t home no one can believe it,
M um and Dad smother me in hugs.

I t is just a dream,
S o, I will make it a reality.

N o one tells me that I can't,
O n the pitch and on a mat,
T oday, I will dream again.

I shall never ever give up,
M e and my dream,
P eople watching
O n a pitch,
S omeone cheering,
S omeone booing,

I don't care because,
B elieve in myself,
L ive a great life
E nd it with a smile.

Olivia Rose Marsh (10)
Kinson Academy, Kinson

Dino Pitch Invaders

One day, at 18:45, Liverpool and United were playing
And the score was 2-0 to Liverpool at half-time
So United had to have a miracle to make a comeback.
Fifteen minutes more, sixty minutes in,
Still 2-0, half an hour left
What will happen?
Five minutes later.
Goal!
United 2-1
Twenty-five minutes left
Goal!
United 2-2
What a game it's been for both.
Don't forget it is UCL Final
So whatever happens, happens.
Eighty-five minutes in five more to go.
Goal, Liverpool.
Just listen to the fans,
They're going mad.
Rashford goes for the shot but
"It's been stopped by a dinosaur, ahhh!"
Run!
Guess Liverpool have won.

Stay safe everyone.
Goodbye.
What a good dream that,
Now time to get ready for school.

Joey Pearce (10)
Kinson Academy, Kinson

A World Full Of Fire!

In my imagination, so wild and free,
There is a world with grass hills and trees,
In that world, there is a child smiling with glee,
That child's name is Lennie,
And he decided to look around,
But you won't believe the thing that he found,
In the distance, smoke rose up,
He ran and ran screaming, "What could it be?"
Once he got there, he saw it was fire,
But then he looked higher and higher,
Flapping its wings, proud as can be,
It was a dragon causing this chaos,
"Come down here," Lennie said bravely,
Once it was down, he didn't know what to say,
But out of nowhere, it just flew away,
When he got home, he told all his friends,
And this is the part where the poem ends.

Lennie King (10)
Kinson Academy, Kinson

The Heaven Dance Of Terror And Happiness

Once upon a dream, in the morning,
The sun shines, and the flowers bloom.
As the wind blows, the trees dance.
As the birds sing, we dance along.

In the grass field, we lie down.
As we look up, the sun strikes and the clouds move.
We look to each other.
We smile as we close our eyes.

We open our eyes to see destruction
And disaster rushing and consuming us
As our nightmares come in.

As we stand up to our nightmare,
We remember to never give up
While fighting our nightmares
To get back to our world of peace.

In the end, we defeat our nightmare.
We both burst out in laughter
As we go to our waterfall to relax,
And we both smile.

Nathan (10)
Kinson Academy, Kinson

Dinos On Isla Nublar

Tails wagging behind them happy as can be,
Looking for their food as far as their eyes can see.
Whether meat or plants they need, majestic they are,
Just be aware or they might crash your car.
Be aware of the T-rexes or even the velociraptors,
Or you might end up dead like the others.
If you see a triceratops running away,
Make sure to get out of the way, or your blood might spill and spray.
Even though herbivores are kind and polite,
Don't anger one or you might end up in a fight.
Near dinos always stay aware,
Even one sudden crack of a stick could send them into a scare.
So make sure you never anger a T-rex, you should never dare,
Or your life just might become unfair.

Paige Harvey (10)
Kinson Academy, Kinson

What Is This Dream?

I had a dream.
A dream you've never had or seen.
Fairies playing around like butterflies, birds flying around in the midnight sky.
One day, I'll wake up,
One day, I'll be a star like Superman or Batman,
I'll have superpowers and fly far.
Maybe if I wake up soon
I will ride the luminous unicorns
And even visit the moon.
I woke up that day
But I wasn't in my room...
I was in a new and scarier town,
Spiders crawling and wizards making potions for doom.
My dream had turned into a nightmare,
Whatever shall I do?
I woke up this time.
I was alive!
People eating and playing around in the blue, blue sky.

Freya Wells (10)
Kinson Academy, Kinson

The Forest

Majestic the forest stands tall and grand,
A hush descends quieting the land.
Peaceful whispers echo through each tree,
Calm and caring the forests decree.

Darkness may linger, a hidden side,
How can we deny what it may hide?
Every corner holds a tale untold,
Naysayers soon in agreement fold.

Boring, they say, a misguided view,
Open your eyes and wonders ensue.
Radient secrets in the shadows reside,
Embracing patience, where truths abide.

Generous mother the forests embrace,
Eternal provider bathes us with grace.
Nurturing us, she feeds us and sings,
Emanating warmth, her maternal wings.

Juliette Sim (8)
Kinson Academy, Kinson

Dragons World

As Skye and Bob settled down to go to sleep after a busy sleepover
They had soon drifted off to sleep then Skye had a dream
She woke up and checked outside to see what the noise was
Then suddenly a dragon blasted Skye!
The dragon picked Skye up
The dragon took Skye to Dragons World
Then flew back for Bob
When Bob woke up and saw he was at Dragons World he screamed
Then they went close to the dragon but they turned out to be mean
One was a fiery red and was chasing Skye and Bob
Then Skye found some fish and distracted the other dragons
Then Skye looked at one that was choking Bob with the fish
And then they became friends.

Skye Morris (9)
Kinson Academy, Kinson

Pixie The Butterfly Fairy

In my dreams, above the sky,
I saw a beautiful butterfly,
Something was off, but I don't know why,
But she was half-human with blue eyes.

She was as light as a feather,
As tough as a tree,
She always said "Hi" to me,
I never wanted the day to end,
Because she was my best friend.

Her name is Pixie, and she is the best,
She always puts herself to the test,
She always made people smile with glee,
As she sat under the old oak tree.

I hope to meet her again,
And maybe she can meet my friends,
I never want this to end,
I will always see my best friend.

Amelia Tyrrell (11)
Kinson Academy, Kinson

Bright Light

That very night,
I saw a bright light.
It bent down to eat,
I thought it was meat.
I brought it a treat,
I went to meet it.

I thought it would rip me,
Instead, it tripped me.
I was shaking in fear,
The creature was rare.
It drooled like rain,
I ran again.

It came closer,
I tiptoed over.
That night I became brave,
I stepped closer, it was a parasite.

I remember the bright light,
It wasn't the parasite,
I wondered what was my first sight,
I woke up in the middle of the night,
I wanted to scream but it was all a dream.

Prince Uchegbu (11)
Kinson Academy, Kinson

Determination And Motivation

To live the life you see,
Be the best that you can be,

Life is full of mountains,
Some are big and some are small,
But if you do not give up,
You can overcome them all,

With great determination comes motivation,
And unleashes your imagination,

Forget the rest, just be your best,

Never give up,
Take a sip out of your confidence cup,

Dream big, reach for the sky,
Turn your aspirations into a high,

Now let's look back as a whole, you have finally reached your end goal,
As we come to the end, share this poem with a friend.

Mia Sandever-Lock (10)
Kinson Academy, Kinson

Little Squeak!

There was a mouse,
In a haunted house,
His name was Little Squeaks,
He was so scared,
His nostrils flared,
And he couldn't even speak.

One day, he got brave,
And came out of his cave,
And said he will not live in fear,
He was now a tough mouse,
Not scared of the house,
And will not even cry one more tear.

It's not what it seems,
It was all in my dreams,
So never be scared, Little Squeak,
He's a fun-loving mouse,
In a beautiful house,
And my story was all tongue-in-cheek.

Maisie Whiffen (8)
Kinson Academy, Kinson

My Dream Life

In my dreams, I'm playing football without a fright,
Never give up, and always be bright,
Sadly, this is a dream; it's not real,
Pretty soon, I will learn how to backheel.

But don't worry, I'm happy,
I hope you're happy; if not, then have some candy,
My family are with me, and they make me smile,
But like a dime.

What is your dream life anyway?
Welcome to mine,
If you never give up,
My story will erupt.

That is mine, how about yours?
And please, never give up.

Ollie Cole (10)
Kinson Academy, Kinson

A Life Living Dream

R oses are red, plums are yum.
O ranges are orange, I love ginger cats.
S tars are booming through the night sky.
E therberries are sweet and yummy too.

B lue is my favourite colour.
L oneliness under a tall tree.
U pside-down cake as silly as can be.
E ggplant, purple my life colour.

Roses are red.
Mangoes are orange.
Bananas are yellow.
Pears are green.
The sky is big and blue.
Eggplants are purple.
Grapefruit is pink.

Isabella Akanbi (7)
Kinson Academy, Kinson

Dream

In the dreamy night, monsters giggle, children play,
But don't worry, the monsters are friendly, okay?
Lights hang as children play, and laughter stays,
He'll take you to the light of effect today.

Pillows like clouds, and clouds like pillows,
Under the moon nine monsters dance, nine sing, nine play instruments,
Is there a monster under your bed?
Don't worry, it's fine if it isn't red,
He is there to protect you, he is there for fun,
Don't run a mile; show love and smile.

Arya Wharton (8)
Kinson Academy, Kinson

My Dream Of Royalty

In my dreams every night
A mansion appears here tonight
And even when I walk inside
It's bright and colourful all around.

This wealth is true
My kindness is infinite
People come to make a bond.

My friends are there, it's them you see
Twirling and swirling everywhere
Scattering all my money and gold
I plead to you now, please stop this world.

At last they stop
Goodbye and farewell
I hear you now
Please stop this spell.

Elsie Shelley (9)
Kinson Academy, Kinson

Rainbow In The Sky

The scene is treetops,
And dreams in your eye,
Baby unicorns flying around the sky,
Fairies jumping up and down,
Penguins swimming sweetly,
Dolphins jumping peacefully,
Candy falling around the trees,
Unicorns playing in the garden,
People getting ice cream,
Birds singing on a palace,
Kids playing in the park,
Princesses reading a book,
Dragons breathing out fire,
What can you see?

Faith Onyinyechukwu (7)
Kinson Academy, Kinson

Sly Fox

A sly fox lived with nature,
The sly fox had no idea who was coming...
Behind him was the pound,
They took him and he escaped in a sly way.

The sly fox hunted its prey in a very sly way,
The sly fox loved running with the wind.
The sly fox stretched as he watched people go by

The sky fox could be cute when he was playing.
The sly fox was as red as fire.

Scarlett Bath (8)
Kinson Academy, Kinson

The Pirates

I went to sea and I saw a tree in the middle
The tall green leaves on the palm
The long dark brown trunk
The sea was as blue as the sky
The ship was as brown as the palm tree trunk
The people on the pirate ship saw another ship
The pirates will sink the ship
They will never give up
They will never stop sailing the sea
They will sail around the world.

Lacey-Jane Watson (8)
Kinson Academy, Kinson

What A Dream

I'm walking in a forest,
Minding my own business,
But then I see Katy Perry,
Ask for a signature,
Then all of a sudden,
It starts heavily snowing, and I'm getting attacked by loads of Vikings,
I'm a bounty to them, apparently,
So they take me in, and I am never seen again.

Seth Read (9)
Kinson Academy, Kinson

Me And My Friend

Me and my friend play all night
When I wake up I say goodbye and wake up and dance
I see my friend, I see my friend forever and ever
I will make new friends
I will miss them when I move on
But I will be part of them
I will always be your friend.

Patience Black (8)
Kinson Academy, Kinson

Me And My Cat

Me and my cat wander the night,
Dancing in the moonlight,
Watching the cars go by,
As the stars shine bright in the sky,
Waiting for morning to rise,
When the dark sky dies,
Finally when the sun is here,
We can go to the cafe near.

Isla Bentley (7)
Kinson Academy, Kinson

Mermaids And Stars

Mermaids live in the sea
What a lovely place to be
Starfish are like the stars so bright
They twinkle at midnight
Glittery scaly tails
Mermaids race with friendly whales
Under the sea dreaming
Sleeping mermaids and me.

Nayana Wright (8)
Kinson Academy, Kinson

The Weather

When in the sun
We have lots of fun
When it rains
It floods our drains
When it snows
We wear extra clothes
When it is lightning
It can be frightening.

Rio Pearce (8)
Kinson Academy, Kinson

Arrival Of A Night Visitor

Here comes the Maniac,
With his dark black gown.
Watching and peering,
Being unfound.

Here comes the Maniac,
His eyes as crimson as blood.
He seeks in the night,
And hides in the day.
He stalks, he scares and never fails
Whilst wearing clothes as dark as the night.

Maniac, Maniac, where did you go?
He is always behind them,
But they never know.

When the children leave their homework behind,
That's when the Maniac comes.
When the children get in the school building,
That's when the Maniac is closer than can be.
When the night is as gloomy as space,
That's when the Maniac has arrived.

He crawls, he runs and catches the kids by surprise.
He scurries, he hides when they see him alive.
So he ventures into the wildness of the night.

Here comes the Maniac,
With his dark black gown.
Watching and peering,
Being unfound.

William Wright (9)
Our Lady's Catholic Primary School, Latchford

The Night Nomad

Here comes the Night Nomad, the gloomy sky sings,
But they sneak past, waving their feather-white wings.

They have piercing eyes like a burning fire,
Teeth as sharp as a piece of wire.
A starry cloak hugs them tight,
In their hand, a lantern, shining bright.

"Night Nomad, Night Nomad, where do you go?"
The people ask, but no one knows.

Here comes the Night Nomad, the gloomy sky sings,
But they sneak past, waving their feather-white wings.

When the stars are dancing in the night sky,
That's when they come,
The children in their beds, they lie,
That's when they come.

They fly free through the fresh air,
They creep past casements without a care,
They swim through flowing streams,
And into the wildness of dreams.

Here comes the Night Nomad, the gloomy sky sings,
But they sneak past, waving their feather-white wings.

Daisy Lowther (9)
Our Lady's Catholic Primary School, Latchford

The Night Owl

Here comes the visitor, echoes as she walks.
Here comes Visator, creeping left and right.

Here comes Visator, moving her feet.
Here comes Visator, black hair in her face.
Here comes Visator, creeping in the woods.
Through the trees and over the leaves.
At midnight that's when they came.

Visator, Visator, who are you?
Visator, Visator, where do you go?
I ask but you don't know.

Walking slowly, walking serenely.
Her tender face waves elegantly in the cold winter breeze.
At midnight that's when they came.
Searching and gleaming, screaming and leaning.
That's when they came.
Her soundless feet float as silver slippers couched on the impaired floor.
Night owl, night owl, where have you been?

Here comes Visator, echoes as she walks.
Here comes Visator moving left and right.

Amellia Jervis (10)
Our Lady's Catholic Primary School, Latchford

Owl Of The Imagination

Here comes the night visitor,
The stars mutter,
Listen close; a hoop-la halo follows you.

Amber hair of her silk feathers almost like the heart of heaven,
Eyes like emeralds as big as a house, and her heart beats like a drum.

Night visitor, night visitor,
Where do you go?
You have to find the beautiful halo.

Here comes the owl, the night visitor calls,
Inky black shadows engulf the air, and that's when she arrives,
No footsteps on the ground, nowhere to be found,
But here comes the night visitor.

She slaps her feathers with a one, two, three,
Out she goes - yippee!
She slides and glides, swirls and twirls,
She flies into the dark abyss of imagination.

Here comes the night visitor, the stars mutter,
Listen close; a hoop-la halo follows you.

Mila Owen (9)
Our Lady's Catholic Primary School, Latchford

The Haunted Night

Here comes ghost girl down the corridor,
She hides and creeps around every corner,
Her eyes are as blank as a sheet of paper,
Her clothes ripped as if a tiger had attacked her,
Her inky, black hair covers her face like strings,
The girl's shoon looked like they came from the sewage.

Ghost girl, ghost girl, where do you hide?
Because we don't see you most of the time.

When the clock strikes midnight, that's when she comes,
She peers through the cabinets,
When the gaudy moon appears, that's when she comes,
She phases up floors and hovers through the corridor,
and she walks into the night sky.

Here comes ghost girl down the corridor,
She hides and creeps around every corner.

Thomas Whewell (10)
Our Lady's Catholic Primary School, Latchford

The Night Visitor Comes

Here comes the visitor,
The stars sing,
Seeing and peering,
In her silvery blue shoon.

Here comes the visitor,
As fast as lightning,
Her eyes like shimmering emeralds,
Her feet soundlessly move,
Her fur is as soft as the fluffy clouds.

Wanderer, Wanderer, where do you go?
The wind howls and the moon shouts.

When the moon is as gaudy as a torch,
That's when the visitors come,
The shadows are moveless,
Moveless houses, moveless mountains,
That's when the visitor comes.

She creeps,
She hides,
She moves and slides,
Into the forest of happiness,
Here comes the visitor,

The stars sing,
Seeing and peering in her silvery blue shoon.

Kira To (9)
Our Lady's Catholic Primary School, Latchford

The Hunter

"Here comes the hunter," the moon sings,
Then he is nowhere to be found again.

Here comes the hunter, as stealthy as a lion, creeping through the forest,
With his soundless feet, his glowing neon green eyes, as moveless shadows slowly tiptoe away.

"Hello hunter, where do you go?" the moon whispers,
The wind shouts.

Above cloudless climes, shadows are like velvet,
Velvet skies, velvet animals, dusty shadows crouched.

He runs as fast as lightning, and stealthily as a fox,
He creeps, he slides, he jumps in the wilderness of dreams.

"Here comes the hunter," the moon sings,
Then he is nowhere to be found again.

Jack Fareham (9)
Our Lady's Catholic Primary School, Latchford

Arrival Of The Night Watcher

Here comes the night watcher; the moon howls,
Peering and seeing the starry skies,
Here comes the night watcher, as stealthy as a cat,
His eyes are like amber owl eyes,
Creeping and searching upon the silver streams.

Hey, night watcher, where do you go?
The moon asks, but the stars know,
When the moon mellows on eloquent stars tenderly,
That's when he comes,
The serene skies guide the way,
That's when he comes.

He hides,
He lurks,
He creeps,
He sneaks through the dark shadows and into your imagination.

Here comes the night watcher; the moon howls,
Peering and seeing the starry skies.

Torin Lam (9)
Our Lady's Catholic Primary School, Latchford

The Night Caller's Call

The night caller wanders the night,
With gaudy eyes shining bright,
His face is covered deep in his cloak,
With dagger-like teeth and a devious smile,
Hands as bony as a skeleton hand,
Upon silver streams, silent whispers float.

Night caller, night caller, where are you?
The stars ask, but the children know.
When the moon looms over the forest, that's when they come,
Their eyes are like glowing embers,
Ember eyes and ember feet; that's when they come.

They slide through trees,
They hover above leaves and into the sky of dreams,
The night caller wanders the night,
With gaudy eyes shining bright.

Angelo Amul (9)
Our Lady's Catholic Primary School, Latchford

The Wanderer

Here comes the Wanderer, the foxes call,
But she does not turn her head
If she hears them at all.
Here comes the Wanderer
As sneaky as a fox,
Eyes like fire,
Her fur like a blanket.
There goes the Wanderer
But where does she go?
Foxes ask, but no one knows,
The stars whisper to the moon,
As the people dance below.
The Wanderer tiptoes through the bushes,
As the birds fly through the night,
And into the forest of imagination,
It's a wonderful sight.
Here comes the Wanderer,
The foxes call,
But she does not turn her head to them
If she hears them at all.

Holly Woodhouse (10)
Our Lady's Catholic Primary School, Latchford

The Night Hopper

Here comes the night hopper
As thin as the wind
"Here he comes," whispers the moon
Only seeing a mahogany brown ear.

Here comes the night hopper
As stealthy as a fox
His feet make no sound
He has amber eyes, leaves crunch on his bare feet
He can hide in milliseconds, that's what he does.

"Night hopper, night hopper, where do you go?"
The moon asks but the stars know.

He comes every full moon not to hunt but to live
When the clocks strike midnight
He comes before you meet him
Just to think do you really want to?

Zachary Walsh (9)
Our Lady's Catholic Primary School, Latchford

The Stalker

Here comes the stalker that shines in moonlight,
Here comes the ghost of hope.

Here she comes with eyes of death,
Hiding in the shadows.
With her silver shoon that glistens in the night,
The hidden figure with bright blonde hair,
Here she comes, the dream bringer.

Stalker, stalker, where do you go?
No one knows, yet no one asks.

When the stars are glistening and the moon is whispering,
The stalker comes through the night,
She creeps, hidden in plain sight,
Yet glides everywhere.

Alice Lee (10)
Our Lady's Catholic Primary School, Latchford

The Wanderer

"Here comes the wanderer," the moon echoes.

Eyes as black as charcoal.
Fangs like daggers.
Scales as hard as obsidian.

"Hello, wanderer. Where do you go?"
The moon asks, but the stars know.

In the cloudless sky, the stars glimmer.
Across the sandy desert, that's when he comes.
In the cool of the desert.
Here comes the wanderer, as quick as the wind.
He shivers with no sand.

"Here comes the wanderer," the moon echoes.

Joel Leicester (10)
Our Lady's Catholic Primary School, Latchford

Arrival Of A Night Visitor

Here comes Anna
The children call
But she doesn't turn her head
If she hears them at all.

Anna's eyes glow like embers
Her skin, like clouds
Her feet make no sound
Anna, why do you search at night?

When the moon is out
That's when Anna comes.
Slowly, silently Anna glides
Through rooms and into houses

Here comes Anna
The children call
But she doesn't turn her head
If she hears them at all.

Sofia Dobson (9)
Our Lady's Catholic Primary School, Latchford

Party, Party All Night

Inspired by 'Diamonds' by Rihanna

Shine bright, shine bright,
So you can be the spotlight,
You can be a disco ball twinkling so bright,
People say, "Go girl, alright!"
People stare at you with pleasure like the stars at night.

People think you are shining, so they shoot you up into the sky like a kite,
Others say, "I'm the best," meaning you're a delight,
I'm like a diamond princess protected by a knight,
I think others see me as an enjoyable sight.

People see me as the best, so I get every party invite,
I am kind and loving, so I can help everyone with excite,
People fly me everywhere on first-class flights.
Party, party all night.

You shine bright like a diamond!

Sienna Pecherska-Brown (10)
St Elizabeths RC Primary School, Belper

The Chocolate House

Reading a book as I drifted off,
With a little sneeze and a cough,
I woke up, confused on the floor,
I looked to my left, at a giant toffee door,
Again to my right, big brother I saw.

We stood up together, getting to our feet,
Me and Dan walked together in the heat,
We walked until we were at the chocolate house,
We skipped up the hill, up to bounce,
For sweets and chocolate, liquorice too.

I just realised we are in the book I was reading,
I told Dan and we ran off, me leading,
I woke up just noticing I was screaming,
My parents rushed in and asked, "What's the matter?"
"Nothing," I told them with a grin on my face.

Erin Clarke (10)
St Elizabeths RC Primary School, Belper

Trapped In My Thoughts

I hear muffled voices screeching for help,
Water crashing against the walls,
I get swept off my feet,
Into a dark room filling up with water.

Crash! Whoosh!
I can't see.
Water up to my neck,
In the distance, I see nine pairs of red eyes charging towards me.

Argh! Eels!
I'm trapped in my thoughts,
Dreaming away,
And then I wake up.

Bronte Lawler (10)
St Elizabeths RC Primary School, Belper

Dreams

As I climbed into bed,
I thought of something in my head,
What are the dreams you have at night?
But then I had a little fright,
I heard a little voice in my room,
My bed started to come alive,
And my bed said,
"Dreams are magical,
Dreams are fun,
Dreams are scary,
Dreams are fierce,
Dreams can be adventurous,
Dreams can be anything."

Mia Groombridge (10)
St Elizabeths RC Primary School, Belper

My Cheeky Pony

My cheeky pony, while I am asleep,
Runs around making out he's a sheep,
He wakes up Mungo (and he's big),
Then he makes all the horses play a game of tig.

Prince and Bailey try to join in,
Those cheeky ponies knock over the bin,
When we go up in the morning,
He pretends he's so sleepy (he's so sly),
Making out he's the peaceful guy.

Meredith James (10)
St Elizabeths RC Primary School, Belper

The Monster Under The Bed

I've read about the monster under the bed
It's always been stuck in my head
But I had the guts to look
If it was real or just in a book
But I saw something move
But I think I spoke too soon
It was just my cat Willow
So I put my head back on my pillow.

Sophie Plastow (11)
St Elizabeths RC Primary School, Belper

Horrible Nightmare

One night I awoke in a small room,
I heard a strange voice say, "Run,"
So I ran as a scary man chased me,
Around the house, through every room,
Through every door, until I was cornered,
Then I woke up, realising it was all just a dream.

Alfie Winter (10)
St Elizabeths RC Primary School, Belper

Joy

J oy is laughter in the air, happiness being spread through love
O thers smiling, spreading peace, meaningful words being said
Y ou frowning, consumed with sadness, listen and learn from this poem.

Orla Skerritt (10)
St Elizabeths RC Primary School, Belper

My Twisted Dream

M y perfect dream, I ride a perfect unicorn
Y ou won't believe what happens next.

T he dream begins in a scary, spooky supermarket
W here there are loads of evil, giggly clowns
I was trying to escape
S ave me! Save me!
T he clowns got me
E vil clowns everywhere
D ance, dance and disappear.

D ance, dance and disappear
R eturning to safety
E nemies disappearing
A ll around sparkling, happy light
M y unicorn is waiting for me.

Indie-Rose Cooke (7)
St John The Baptist CE (VA) Primary School, Pebmarsh

The Footballer Through The Ages

There was once a footballer,
The footballer was young,
The footballer was suddenly in his teenage years,
He pelted the ball into the direction of the wall,
Bang, crash, thump!
The ball crashed onto the floor,
He was now an adult,
His silky skills meant he would score every chance he got,
One day as usual the ball crashed into the net,
But in the third minute, his third goal came,
Suddenly, he was elderly,
So that meant no more football,
No more football,
Then no more him.

Baxter Croton (8)
St John The Baptist CE (VA) Primary School, Pebmarsh

Halloween Nightmare!

In my dream at Halloween, I see a haunted house.
I go inside.
I find sweets on the table.
A door slams and I jump in fright.
Then I see a giant guinea pig, my biggest enemy!
His name is Boris and he has an army of guinea pigs behind him!
I run upstairs and find a door, quickly I run inside.
There is a bed and I hide under it.
I hear footsteps coming up the stairs.
I'm feeling so scared!
I shut my eyes.
I open my eyes.
I'm in my bed - it was just a dream!

Teddy Andress (8)
St John The Baptist CE (VA) Primary School, Pebmarsh

Darkness In A Room

I wake up in a room, dark, dull, depressing.
I open the old red door. It slams behind me with a bang!
I see nothing but darkness. Is this a dream?
I hear the creak of a floorboard.
I feel like a mouse in a trap, lost and helpless.
I take one hello.
I feel alone, but I'm sure I'm not.
I am scared.
I think it's time to wake up.
I am not scared anymore.
I can't believe it: Was it a dream, or was it not?

Lana (9)
St John The Baptist CE (VA) Primary School, Pebmarsh

The Wizard

I was in a dark, dark corridor.
A wizard with a long black cloak and black hat.
With eyes like balls of fire.
I stepped back for a place to hide.
My worst fear was walking towards me.
They had an evil smile on their face.
I thought it was a joke.
I ran as fast as I could.
The wizard ran faster and faster and faster!
I wanted someone to help me.
I woke up snug as a bug in my bed. Yes, yes, yes.

Ophelia Creamer (8)
St John The Baptist CE (VA) Primary School, Pebmarsh

A Winter's Night

Nothing has prepared me for this moment,
I could not see anything; it was as dark as a winter's night,
It was so cold I thought I had frostbite, but with might, I powered through,
Then I heard from the shadows a mighty thump thump,
I could hear it getting closer, *thump thump,*
I could see it and it said, "Time for school,"
"What?" I said,
Then I woke up and it was a dream.

Arlo Bennet (9)
St John The Baptist CE (VA) Primary School, Pebmarsh

Halloween Nightmares

Every night in October, a nightmare floods into my head.
I find myself trapped in a haunted house, surrounded by cobwebs.
As I walk through a corridor,
Something scuttles across the floor.
I suddenly see a shadow with eight legs.
It's a massive spider.
Wow, lots of massive, hairy spiders appear.
The bats laugh.
I close my eyes tightly and reopen them.
It was just a nightmare.

Toby Digby (8)
St John The Baptist CE (VA) Primary School, Pebmarsh

Fat Pet Pig

My favourite dream is of a pig
My pig is joyful, he is pink and brown
He is my pet, his name is Balon
All around, pink trotters dancing
Sugary sweets, chocolate treats
Chomp! Chomp! Chomp!
My pig loves to eat, bigger and bigger he grows
Like a giant balloon
He won't stop growing.
It's getting rather funny.
I can't stop laughing.

Frank Starckey Gammons (8)
St John The Baptist CE (VA) Primary School, Pebmarsh

Guinea Pig Dreams

G nawing on some tasty treats,
U sing the warm, spotty bed,
I nside tunnels, they love to hide,
N ibbling fresh hay,
E very day, they run and play,
A lways giving the best hugs.

P iggies are the perfect pet,
I go out there every morning,
G uineas are the best; you could never wish for better.

Fleur Amos (7)
St John The Baptist CE (VA) Primary School, Pebmarsh

Haunted House

I was in a haunted house and the door shut and locked
So I had to find a way out
I saw a hatch so I went down
A big colony of bats flew at my head
They opened their mouths and I quickly shut the hatch
And sat down and took a breath
Then I saw a shield covered in cobwebs
So I scraped them off so I went down
And got free and then I woke up.

Louis Brown (8)
St John The Baptist CE (VA) Primary School, Pebmarsh

Fright Night

A night so bright,
I fear with fright,
I bear to dread tonight,
Death may strike in the name of bite,
And may not be bright,
Pirates, ghosts, name them all, they will come tonight.

I dread to think what they shall bring,
Daggers, swords or just pure might,
Yes, yes, yes, yes, scary tonight.

Griff Williamson (8)
St John The Baptist CE (VA) Primary School, Pebmarsh

The Eiffel Tower

In my dream, I was in France,
I saw the Eiffel Tower and I was with my mummy,
I was happy,
Suddenly someone jumped off the Eiffel Tower,
It was the Grinch!
I was scared!
The Grinch was going to take over the Eiffel Tower!
I woke up in my bed!
It was just a dream!

Olivia Head (8)
St John The Baptist CE (VA) Primary School, Pebmarsh

Magic Night

Unicorns bouncing from cloud to cloud shining into the night sky
Hooves trot softly and smoothly, not leaving a cloud in two.
Lighting up the night sky.
Hooves drop shimmering stars.
Maybe a star will land too.
You might be lucky to see one land into the magical land below.

Finley Smith (9)
St John The Baptist CE (VA) Primary School, Pebmarsh

Upside-Down Houses

In my dreams every night, I see upside-down floating houses made of animal fur
So I open the door and see upside-down tables and upside-down food
I walk along and see floating stairs, I try to walk up them but I can't
I see animal fur beds so I go and lie on it and open my eyes.

Edie Short (7)
St John The Baptist CE (VA) Primary School, Pebmarsh

Flying

F abulous things I can see down below
L ying on a cloud I can see an art studio
Y ou and me having fun in the sky
I feel like a bird
N othing can stop me now
G liding through the air with my dog by my side.

Robyn Porter (8)
St John The Baptist CE (VA) Primary School, Pebmarsh

Unicorn Dreams

I have a unicorn that loves me.
Every night it sleeps with me.
My unicorn will stay with me.
I feel calm and safe.
I will stay in the castle always.
I'm lucky to have a unicorn.
I love my unicorn.

Saffron Howard (8)
St John The Baptist CE (VA) Primary School, Pebmarsh

The Big Dream

In my favourite dream,
I saw enormous show jumps,
The shining gold cup,
Black, blue, red, yellow, green, purple,
In I go, my life depends on this,
Clear! I was so joyful.

Rosie George (8)
St John The Baptist CE (VA) Primary School, Pebmarsh

I'm Flying In Space

I'm lying in bed and what do I see? I'm in a rocket flying free
I look out the window to see an alien spaceship chasing after me
I'm dashing and darting past all sorts of planets
It's time to bring out our supersonic gadget!

With our super blaster loaded here it goes
With one big blow, the egg hits its nose!
With my loyal pet doggie called Tommy by my side
I think to myself, *this is a crazy ride!*

With a *bang* on the roof and a *thud* down below
To my surprise, I stub my toe
My bodyguard, Bob, says, "The aliens are here"
And says nothing more and runs off in fear

I creep and I creep and then open the door
And to my surprise, it is aliens galore!
As soon as one is about to reach my head
I find myself waking up in bed.

Archie Dykes (10)
The Manor CE Primary School, Coalpit Heath

The Green

Day done
Lie down in my bed
Close my eyes and
Rest my head.

Enter a world
So lush and clean.
Rainbow of flowers,
Leaves broad and green.

Market in full swing,
Perfume and spice,
Merchants selling silks,
Children rolling dice.

I try to join them,
But I'm stuck.
Vines curl around my ankle,
Just my luck.

Vines tight at my leg,
They climb up my spine,
And drag me down.
We are gone in no time.

Leafy tendrils at my neck,
I yell my desperate pleas.
All is green.
No one hears; nobody sees.

If you find yourself
Dozing or taking a nap,
Beware, the market is bait,
And the green is a trap.

Anouska King (10)
The Manor CE Primary School, Coalpit Heath

Terror Of The Night

T rembling, you let out a shriek
E verything around you makes you feel meek
R ushing down the stairs that guide you through
R estless feelings that seem quite new
O ut of the blue
R attling armour terrifies you.

O minous sensations in the room you're now in
F ear breaching the top of your skin.

T he beast in front of thee
H owling like a banshee
E verything merged into one.

N othing can shake your numb feeling
I gniting a candle to see your foe
G oosebumps settle as you come to know
H owever, you come to see
T he scuttling rodent in front of thee.

Isaac Beech (11)
The Manor CE Primary School, Coalpit Heath

Butterflies

B eautiful insects in the sky
U nique animals flying
T rying to help the bees make me sneeze
T aking to pollen my eyes are swollen
E xploring different flowers smelling and
R eady for sharing any kinds of powders
F or wildlife creatures and any other flowers
L arvae is the start then fluffy caterpillars is another part
I nto colourful and bright butterflies they become
E ast or west, north or south, their wings are fluttering now
S o this is the end of this lovely poem where I was telling you about butterflies and pollen.

Ana De Oliveira Calvo (10)
The Manor CE Primary School, Coalpit Heath

In The Sky

Up in the sky, I fly very high,
I soar like a kite on a fine summer's night,
So many sights I see in my life,
What is that light so blinding and bright?
A unicorn, a fairy, Santa possibly?
I know, I know a star indeed,
If I could join that star over there,
Down upon the world I would stare,
A star in the daytime, how can that be?
Do you feel lucky to see it just like me?
Me and this star, we are so close,
A friendship that is better than most,
And when I go inside for tea,
I know she'll still be there waiting for me.

Molly Flay (9)
The Manor CE Primary School, Coalpit Heath

Magical Land

Once upon a time, I had a dream,
To write the best poem ever seen...

In this beautiful land with towering trees,
Birds, blossom, leaves and bees.
The dew glistened in the rising sun,
The morning madness had begun.
Animals scampered to and fro,
Some toppled over like a domino.
Busy bees, tweeting birds,
(They were making a choir I heard)
As the morning quietened down,
My frown was turned upside down!

Daniel Farr (10)
The Manor CE Primary School, Coalpit Heath

Dragons

I was not ready for this place I see,
There was no one from my family.
I tried not to cry and to be brave,
But then I realised I was in a cave.

Then there was something out of sight.
What was there was really a fright.
I stopped for a second to look and see,
But then there was a dragon near me.

I cry to my mum, "Mum! Mum!"
And then I woke up with a broken thumb.

Arthur Parsons (9)
The Manor CE Primary School, Coalpit Heath

In A Galaxy

In a galaxy full of stars
I could see them from afar
Lights shooting across the sky
They had caught me in the corner of my eye
Thousands of planets spread around
I couldn't hear a single sound
Gazing around the galaxy
There was so much more to see.

Emily Smith (9)
The Manor CE Primary School, Coalpit Heath

Sound

As the silver moon starts to rise,
I close my tired, sleepless eyes,
I drift off to sleep and start to dream,
While on my face shines a single moonbeam.

I find myself in a distant land,
With gentle waves and golden sand,
The cool evening breeze brushes my skin,
Then, in the distance, I hear a bone-crushing din.

The sound creeps to a violent growl,
A mind-bending roar and an ear-piercing howl,
Covering my ears, I fall to the ground,
Shaking, I'm slowly flattened by the sound.

I thrust my eyes open, heart pounding fast,
Realising how many hours have passed,
As my breathing slows down, I realise it was something I dreamed,
Despite how real the whole thing seemed.

Ruby Imuere (10)
Westcourt Primary School, Gravesend

Your Dream

F uture is near, all goals are within arm's reach
U nique dreams, everyone has, only yours can be met by you
T antamount dreams are what yours are
U mpteen dreams you might have, all possible of achieving
R each for your goals, and never give up
E ven if you don't meet your dreams soon, you have a lifetime to meet them.

V oices from the park get louder each day
A ttend to your people, show live
N ever give up, even though it's hard.

L ifetime ends; enjoy
I t while it lasts
F amily grows like love; don't stop, but shine
E nter the darkness all alone.

Micheline Agyarko (11)
Westcourt Primary School, Gravesend

The Nightmare

In my dreams every night,
There is a creature that gives me a fright.
Its laugh and glare is quite a scare.
It chases me every night.
It feels like I will never see light.
I close my eyes and then open them.
It seems that the creature is not there.
I turn around and see smoke.
I really hope this is a joke!
The creature lures me into a shed,
It is painted red.
That is when I realise it is going to chop off my head!
I scream so loud.
Suddenly, I am back in my bed.
My mother comes into the room.
She asks if I am okay; I don't respond.
I only look out of the window
And the creature waves hello!

Anna-Luisa Souza Garcez (11)
Westcourt Primary School, Gravesend

Many Dreams

Many dreams there are,
Some seem impossible, some too far,
I could be a footballer, scoring goals in my sleep,
Earning money every minute, all in a heap.

I could be a doctor, helping with care,
Dealing with diseases, discovering cures so rare.
Maybe a racer, *vroom, vroom*, I'm away!
I'm just a blur, nothing in my way.

What about astronomy, spying the night sky?
Finding stars so bright, up so high.
I'm not sure, maybe I'll wait,
Let's just see, and I'll meet my fate,
Oh, I wonder what awaits.

Zayn Shiyamin (11)
Westcourt Primary School, Gravesend

The Night Terror

As daylight vanished,
The night's terror began,
With horror on my face,
I turned the light off...

Dark, eerie ghosts,
Piercing through walls like the colour of moss,
Is this a dream?
Tick, tick, tick, tick, tick...

Boom! Lightning flashed less than a second,
A glimpse of bloodthirsty ghosts surrounding me,
Tick, tick, tick, tick, tick, tick,
As they bit me I...

As I gasped,
I realised I...
Was on my bed.

Swettha Vallathan (11)
Westcourt Primary School, Gravesend

Memories

My head was spinning and my vision was a blur,
As I sat up in the darkness, I wondered what would occur.
Before I knew it, the place had turned bright,
My eyes couldn't handle it, so I shut them tight.
I gasped as hundreds of pictures surrounded me,
Where even am I? What could this be?
To my surprise, my wonderful parents appeared,
I had seen myself, which made me feel weird.
My eyes widened, full of realisation,
As I watched my memories with a joyful sensation.

Saaruja Granavel (10)
Westcourt Primary School, Gravesend

Nightmares

N othing has prepared me for this strange land.
I nvisible monsters make me jump,
G iants bigger than skyscrapers.
H ow did I get here? This must be a nightmare.
T *hud!* Something moves closer to me.
M onsters feast in the nighttime.
A bandoned houses in an unknown forest!
R eaching claws, scratching the old door,
E vil horses crushing me on the bed.
S uddenly, I wake up in my bed and go back to sleep.

Ayse Koksal (11)
Westcourt Primary School, Gravesend

Football

F orever, I will always love football
O ver and over again, I have a dream to be a professional
O ne day, I hope it comes true and I imagine playing for Arsenal
T hinking every day, wishing I would make it
B esides having another dream, my heart is set on football
A ll night dreaming, at least hoping, to go to a stadium
L ove for football can never be explained
L oving watching football, every minute, loving it.

Oyinda Soremekun (11)
Westcourt Primary School, Gravesend

When I Grow Up

When I grow up, I would like to be a beauty influencer.
I want to make people feel beautiful.
I want to change people's lives.
I want everyone to have perfect skin.
I want everyone's skin to shine like the golden stars that brighten the sky.
I want all the clients that I get when I am older to have the best skin,
And know that they are worth a million with their brand-new skin!

Shayla-Mai Adam (11)
Westcourt Primary School, Gravesend

Formula One

In the world of dreams,
The cars zoom like lightning,
The sweat always dripping,
Wheels are being exchanged every second.
And being pumped by energizing fuel,
The racing cars are ready and the people too,
The crowds cheer like a screaming hyena,
And the cars zoom like a cheetah,
The pressure held is like a meteor ready to smash,
But waking up is like being last.

Sajjad Madadi (10)
Westcourt Primary School, Gravesend

Mazes

As I enter this mysterious place,
I am sucked into the eternal void,
I cannot let go,
I have to walk towards it,
Openings to more paths but this one intrigues me,
Darkness takes over,
I cannot see where I am,
"Keep walking," I tell myself,
Then I am met with an amazing thing,
A portal that takes me to my most magnificent dreams.

Lewis Watson (11)
Westcourt Primary School, Gravesend

My Horror Dream

No one ever prepared me for this monstrosity of a horror dream.

Clowns chasing me down the stairs,
The stench of a million corpses rotting throughout the air,
Evil eagles attacking innocent bears,
Gargantuan monsters roaming the earth, giving everyone eerie glares.

This is only a nightmare,
I must not let it get to me.

Reggie Jones (11)
Westcourt Primary School, Gravesend

Candy Land

I had a dream of a world full of sweets
With a chocolate fountain full of marshmallows
And cookies and whipped cream
Just perfect for making smores
The sweets came alive, big and small
The sun was smiling down and melting
The marshmallows just perfectly.
Having fun, riding around while eating fruits.
And then I woke up.

Aniyah Campbell (11)
Westcourt Primary School, Gravesend

Spider

S piders, scary arachnids scuttling around,
P etrifying students on the school grounds,
I think my death is soon to arrive,
D eafening screams halt, *am I alive?*
E verything stops, no spiders or school, nothing can be seen,
R emember, *phew*, I'm awake and it was just a dream.

Charlotte Hatch (11)
Westcourt Primary School, Gravesend

O Monstro Sem Fim

Many dark noises at night.
A monster on the right?
No one will help me.
I will have to wake up!
Running and running, from a monster catching me.
A killer?
Or a friend?
Fortunately, I woke up.
I ran and ran to Mum.
Nobody was there...
Apparently, the nightmare is here!
No one will help me.

Klayver Santos Costa (11)
Westcourt Primary School, Gravesend

My Future

I could be a nurse,
Destroy a heavily unwanted curse.
I could be a dancer,
Jump and twirl, be the world's best prancer,
No this isn't right,
I could be a knight that could feature kills,
Or a teacher with excellent skills.
I will help to educate the young,
Oh, I wish to be a teacher one day!

Cerys Mannerings (10)
Westcourt Primary School, Gravesend

Lost Again

L ight left the Earth,
O h, I'm trapped,
S uddenly I'm all alone,
T he presence of another body.

A gain, I'm lost,
G awping at the darkness,
A manic creature stands before me,
I want to escape,
N ow I need out.

Skye Sambrook (11)
Westcourt Primary School, Gravesend

Candy Lane

I fell in a world with candies and lollipops
With chocolates that make you pop
Candies and cotton candies
Chocolates and biscuits
Chocolate valves and milky streams
Almost everything was a dream
Flowers and houses made out of chocolates
I must eat everything
Before it's too late!

Tomilola Olusola-Taiwo (10)
Westcourt Primary School, Gravesend

Makeup Influencer

I wish to become a makeup influencer,
I wish to make people feel beautiful,
I wish for people to fall in love with makeup,
I wish for faces to glow,
I wish for people to care and be fair,
I wish for customers to come through the door,
During these times at three and four.

Lexi Kay (10)
Westcourt Primary School, Gravesend

A Twist

In my dreams every night,
Stars burn bright,
Fairies galore,
Goblins in sight,
Leprechauns dancing in the light,
Some fight over gold to claim their rights,
I've finally got a place to stay,
But every dream has its faults,
This one is I'm getting lost.

Saisha Joshi (10)
Westcourt Primary School, Gravesend

Noises Everywhere

D aydreams or dreams in my bed,
R ainbow bed sheets keep me warm at night,
E avesdropping on my parents while I lay,
A ny kind of noise could wake me,
M any foxes outside tapping on the window,
S o many noises I can't have a slumber.

Deimante Pranskeviciute (11)
Westcourt Primary School, Gravesend

My Nightmare

I could never be prepared for my nightmare,
Disturbing clowns coming from the darkest alleys,
Gigantic spiders waiting to pounce,
Massive monsters waiting to be fed,
The witch hiding under the bed,
Getting lost when the sun sets,
Was it ever going to end?

Jessica Buckland (10)
Westcourt Primary School, Gravesend

Animals

A nimals surround me
N othing but love surrounds the animals
I am a vet
M y hands fascinated by what they can feel
A mazed by what I can see
L ove spreads throughout the vet clinic
S pecial animals in my care.

Ivy Jean Foreman (10)
Westcourt Primary School, Gravesend

Actress

A chieve your dreams
C hase your true ambitions
T ell the tale of your story
R each for your imagination
E very second matters
S hooting stars light your way
S tay strong while the spotlight shines on you.

Lilian Nwokorobia (11)
Westcourt Primary School, Gravesend

Dreams

D reams are infinite.
R eading helps your creativity, imagine them.
E very dream has its own meaning.
A dream is like a scene playing in your head.
M eeting your dreams isn't important, it's about your imagination.

Polina Kovalenko (10)
Westcourt Primary School, Gravesend

Vet Helper

In my dreams every night I dream of,
Me being a vet,
Looking after pets,
Having no rest,
Non-stop mess,
Helping pets,
All day long,
Making more mess,
It never stops,
Saving animals' lives is hard.

Preciouslily Mulvihill (11)
Westcourt Primary School, Gravesend

I Want To Be A Beauty Influencer

I want to be a beauty influencer,
Someone who films beauty products,
I want to be a beauty influencer,
Someone who helps products grow,
I want to be a beauty influencer,
That's why I want to be a beauty influencer.

Libby Miller (10)
Westcourt Primary School, Gravesend

The Rugby Field

Tackled to the ground,
Studs digging through the fresh flesh,
Blood running down my face,
Playing on until the end,
Not stopping the adrenaline,
Facing those obstacles,
The whistle's been blown...

Austen Winn-Gordon (10)
Westcourt Primary School, Gravesend

Dream

D reaming all night long
R eal ponies and horses
E ating candy and food and sweets
A s athletes are practising and playing sports
M onsters hiding, ready to attack enemies.

Stefan Poiana (11)
Westcourt Primary School, Gravesend

The Night

P eaceful times
I nside a new world
L ying in a comfy bed
L odged in a deep sleep
O vernight dreaming about goals
W aking up in a new world.

Haaris Samuel (11)
Westcourt Primary School, Gravesend

Dream

D reamy dragons high above
R ivers splash through the forest
E erie sights in the trees
A pproaching dangers
M alicious piranhas waiting for a target.

Kymami Saddler (10)
Westcourt Primary School, Gravesend

Ocean Sea

In my dream, I can see,
A piercing blue ocean sea,
There's a noise I can hear,
And it's coming from below here,
In my dream, I can see,
A piercing red ocean sea.

Imogen Clarke (11)
Westcourt Primary School, Gravesend

I Don't Want To Wake

I fly high soaring in the sky,
I go faster than a rocket,
I run quicker than a race car,
I jump higher than a cloud,
But I cannot read,
I cannot do a simple task.

Harry Rose (10)
Westcourt Primary School, Gravesend

Bunny

I had a dream!
It was sunny when I saw a bunny
Hopping up and down,
With a scream, eating some cream.
The bunny seems happy
But why was he wearing a nappy?

Nimrat Kambaj (11)
Westcourt Primary School, Gravesend

I Had A Dream

I had a dream,
Where the bright lights gleam,
It's magical but tragical,
And while the sun rises and shines,
The cold disappears and dies.

Jessica Kiskyte (10)
Westcourt Primary School, Gravesend

Sea

S weet dreams in your mind,
L ost in the sea,
E nd is far,
E nd is near,
P en you will write the end.

Dennis Daukste (11)
Westcourt Primary School, Gravesend

Ronaldo

R onaldo
O bjects
N ight
A pple phone
L ying down
D ream
O f Fortnite.

Guiseppe Forzani (11)
Westcourt Primary School, Gravesend

Sleep

S leep
L ying
E ating
E lectricity
P illow.

Jake Ned (10)
Westcourt Primary School, Gravesend

Dancing Horse

There once was a horse that dreamt of dancing,
Everyone laughed at her when she was out prancing,
Every day she thought, *why do I keep dancing on my own?*
I love to dance, but I'm sad that I'm alone.

Her rider would come and she would be all excited,
When they flew through the wind, she would feel delighted,
But when she was left in the field back at home,
She missed her rider so much, she would constantly roam.

One day she heard noises, a motor at the gate,
It was her rider, she just couldn't wait,
But then on the air, a whinnying sound,
That echoed in the field, and the trees all around.

Suddenly bucking and jumping around,
Another horse running and kicking the ground,
She ran towards her, a new friend to be known,
At last, at last she was no longer alone.

Day after day, around the field they pranced,
And happily ever after they playfully danced.

Nyra Potts (9)
Willand School, Willand

Me And My Mum's Night-time Adventures

My mum and I have a special place
We meet in our dreams and I see her face
Off to Unicorn Land we go
For a night-time of wonder and glow
There are sparkling unicorns to ride
We fly through the sky and glide
Colourful candyfloss and magical sparkly sweets
We make snow angels and hear the birds tweet
What fun we have on the twisty-turny slides
We land at the bottom with a great big collide
I wake in the morning with a smile on my face
As my mum kisses my cheek, saying, "That was a fun race."

Rosie Luker (9)
Willand School, Willand

Dream Flowers

It was a warm summer's day,
And the sun was out to play.
The flowers looked up to the sun,
I could tell this day was going to be fun.
I was flying up high,
In the big blue sky.
I heard the flowers talking,
So I decided to start walking.
The flowers said, "What's your name?"
Then we decided to play a game.
Oh what fun we had, we even had ice cream,
But then I woke up and it was a dream.

Rosie Whitehead (9)
Willand School, Willand

Wizard Duel

I am dreaming of wizards with wands,
Their bonds, as they duel with their
Wands, flashes of light red and green
Quite bright!

I see wizards on brooms,
As they zigzag through the
Ink-black sky, chasing witches
Who might meet their *doom!*

Then, *boom*: a witch and a wizard soar overhead.
Am I still in my bed? Hit by a curse, I scream.
Luckily, it's just a dream.

Holly Isobel James (10)
Willand School, Willand

YOUNG WRITERS INFORMATION

We hope you have enjoyed reading this book – and that you will continue to in the coming years.

If you're a young writer who enjoys reading and creative writing, or the parent of an enthusiastic poet or story writer, do visit our website **www.youngwriters.co.uk**. Here you will find free competitions, workshops and games, as well as recommended reads, a poetry glossary and our blog.

If you would like to order further copies of this book, or any of our other titles, then please give us a call or visit **www.youngwriters.co.uk**.

Young Writers
Remus House
Coltsfoot Drive
Peterborough
PE2 9BF
(01733) 890066
info@youngwriters.co.uk

YoungWritersUK **YoungWritersCW**
youngwriterscw **youngwriterscw**